G-CE
361.61

NEW DIRECTIONS FOR EVALUATION

N532

no. 90

Sponsored by the American Evaluation Association

Editorial Policy and Procedures

New Directions for Evaluation, a quarterly sourcebook, is an official publication of the American Evaluation Association. The journal publishes empirical, methodological, and theoretical works on all aspects of evaluation. A reflective approach to evaluation is an essential strand to be woven through every volume. The editors encourage volumes that have one of three foci: (1) craft volumes that present approaches, methods, or techniques that can be applied in evaluation practice, such as the use of templates, case studies, or survey research; (2) professional issue volumes that present issues of import for the field of evaluation, such as utilization of evaluation or locus of evaluation capacity; (3) societal issue volumes that draw out the implications of intellectual, social, or cultural developments for the field of evaluation, such as the women's movement, communitarianism, or multiculturalism. A wide range of substantive domains is appropriate for *New Directions for Evaluation;* however, the domains must be of interest to a large audience within the field of evaluation. We encourage a diversity of perspectives and experiences within each volume, as well as creative bridges between evaluation and other sectors of our collective lives.

The editors do not consider or publish unsolicited single manuscripts. Each issue of the journal is devoted to a single topic, with contributions solicited, organized, reviewed, and edited by a guest editor. Issues may take any of several forms, such as a series of related chapters, a debate, or a long article followed by brief critical commentaries. In all cases, the proposals must follow a specific format, which can be obtained from the editor-in-chief. These proposals are sent to members of the editorial board and to relevant substantive experts for peer review. The process may result in acceptance, a recommendation to revise and resubmit, or rejection. However, the editors are committed to working constructively with potential guest editors to help them develop acceptable proposals.

Jennifer C. Greene, Coeditor-in-Chief
Department of Educational Psychology
University of Illinois
260E Education Building
1310 South Sixth Street
Champaign, IL 61820
e-mail: jcgreene@uiuc.edu

Gary T. Henry, Coeditor-in-Chief
School of Policy Studies
Georgia State University
P.O. Box 4039
Atlanta, GA 30302-4039
e-mail: gthenry@gsu.edu

CONTENTS

EDITOR'S NOTES

Public sector interventions designed to improve the lives of citizens have a long history. The astounding growth of such efforts in the past thirty-five years has led to widespread interventions in health, education, criminal justice, labor training, and other social services that might have been unimaginable to our grandparents' generation. These interventions have served as an engine of challenge for those of us who, as evaluation specialists, ask whether a particular public program is achieving its goal and whether there are better ways to manage certain public services.

Inevitably policymakers have developed their sense of how best to improve the quality of citizens' lives. For example, in the medical community, a common wisdom is that targeted prevention programs for various diseases offer the best chance to prevent them. In education, a common wisdom is developing that testing and accountability will improve student performance. As a third example, wealthier citizens increasingly are buying private education for their children, private recreation for their families, and private security services for their homes. Thus, a common wisdom is developing that such opting out of the public sector should free up more public resources for the remaining 80 percent of citizens who continue to rely on public services.

Are these common wisdoms correct? The chapters that follow demonstrate how evaluation evidence can overturn widely held intuitions. Rosemary Chalk, Joel Garner, and Michael Stoto show in their chapters that public policies for reducing recidivism for domestic violence and reducing perinatal transmission of HIV have been restructured dramatically because of findings from evaluations. Jennifer Light offers compelling historical evidence of how assumptions that privatization will lead to reduced demands for public services are exactly backward when applied to home security systems. David Pillemer, Henry Levin, Edward Miech, Bill Nave, and Frederick Mosteller describe how evaluators can offer insights to practicing educators that contradict a common wisdom.

Several features of this volume make the cumulative impact of the findings especially compelling. First, most of the authors have rich and extensive evaluation experience. Several present evaluation findings using methods that are, for them, unexpected. For example, Mosteller has specialized for half a century in gathering experimental evidence, yet his chapter relies heavily on in-depth case studies. This is a testament to an expert evaluator's willingness to be open to multiple methods of analysis, where needs of policymakers often shape what form of evaluation evidence they will find most compelling.

A second appealing feature of these chapters as a group is that each turns up a surprise, and the surprises span several disciplines. The chapters view evaluation from the lenses of history, health care, epidemiology, economics, psychology, and education. Their cumulative effect clearly transcends any parochial details of one discipline.

A third compelling feature comes from the different forms of evidence the authors use. This volume contains examples of randomized field trials, historical analyses from archival sources, and ethnographic evaluations using case studies.

The common theme is the importance of doing in-depth, defensible work regardless of methodology. When this level of care is used, evaluation results can change public policies, as several chapters illustrate. In health care, domestic violence prevention, and education, interventions in the coming years will be different from interventions that were considered ideal in past years. These changes suggest that policymakers often welcome evidence from the evaluation community and are willing to change their policies based on that evidence. Policymakers especially welcome compelling, defensible evidence that is actionable and challenges a long-established common wisdom. It helps them to do their jobs more effectively. As a result, everyone, from taxpayers to program recipients, is better served.

Richard J. Light
Editor

RICHARD J. LIGHT is professor of education at the Harvard Graduate School of Education and the Kennedy School of Government. He is chair of the Changing Demographics in Colleges Project at the American Academy of Arts and Sciences.

An underappreciated opportunity for evaluators is to develop compelling, defensible, empirical findings that challenge a common wisdom. Policymakers are often highly receptive to such new insights.

Evaluating to Resolve Controversies

Richard J. Light

The six chapters in this volume offer six examples of using evaluation methods to resolve a policy controversy. Each tackles a prominent policy question, and in just about every case, this question has had a widely accepted common wisdom. Each chapter then illustrates how a particular evaluation method was helpful for resolving its debate. The chapters offer yet another strength: an illustration of how this work can clarify policymakers' understanding of trade-offs they must confront when choosing a course of action in different social arenas.

As a collection, the chapters share one overarching appealing feature: they reach a conclusion that was not obvious to most policymakers in advance. Put another way, each comes up with a finding that many readers may find somewhat surprising. This matters because evaluation as a field has made extraordinary progress. Old arguments, such as the merits of quantitative versus qualitative evaluations and the virtues and limitations of randomized, experimental designs, have now been widely debated and largely resolved. Discussion in the field has evolved toward a far more constructive agreement that each method has great value when used appropriately. There is even broad agreement that multiple methods can work well together and provide complementary kinds of evidence in examining a complex policy challenge. Old arguments about whether meta-analysis and data syntheses are a major step forward, or a mindless combining of apples and oranges, have been superseded by constructive examples of where a careful meta-analysis has been helpful in education, health, criminal justice, welfare, and medicine. Readers will easily add other examples.

NEW DIRECTIONS FOR EVALUATION, no. 90, Summer 2001   © Jossey-Bass, A Publishing Unit of John Wiley & Sons, Inc.   3

This volume also illustrates several fruitful areas where all evaluators can pursue further work. Following are five concrete examples, each illustrated by at least one of the following chapters:

• How do we interpret conflicting findings from several evaluations of a similar program or intervention? It is rare for multiple evaluations of similar programs to find consistently positive or negative effects. Some conflicting findings inevitably emerge. One response to such conflict is to throw our hands up in frustration and agree that social science research, often full of conflict, rarely answers questions in a systematic way. I urge that we do exactly the opposite. Conflicting findings offer an opportunity to learn from additional evidence. Conflicts help us to understand, for example, that although the main effect of a treatment might be positive, some subgroups of recipients of that treatment may respond negatively and in a predictable way. Ultimately if we view conflicting outcomes among evaluations as an opportunity to learn what treatment works best for whom, when, and under what circumstances, the conflicting findings across evaluations will become an unexpected benefit to policymakers.

Chapter Two by Rosemary Chalk and Joel Garner illustrates that conflicting findings can be capitalized on in a positive way, even when they surprise policymakers. Chalk and Garner examine what evaluations reveal about effective strategies for dealing with domestic violence: physical assault, rape, and threats such as stalking or physical harassment. A special feature of this chapter is the way the authors chronicle the accumulation of evidence from well-designed evaluations. They point out how the willingness of evaluators to consider unexpected findings as real rather than spurious was critical to the evaluation process.

Chalk and Garner begin by describing the first randomized experiment examining domestic abuse, conducted in Minneapolis in 1984. It led police departments around the nation to decide that arrest of a perpetrator is the most effective deterrent policy. Yet five follow-up studies (in Omaha, Nebraska; Charlotte, North Carolina; Milwaukee, Wisconsin; Dade County, Florida; and Colorado Springs, Colorado) turned up different, and unexpected, results, which Chalk and Garner describe in detail. Each study over time presented a new building block, and their cumulative effect was to change policies away from arrest of the perpetrator to other strategies.

This chapter illustrates how evaluations designed using traditional, randomized plans led, because of the conflicting outcomes, to a cumulative evolution in policies to reduce repeated domestic violence. Chalk and Garner's argument links well with Jennifer Light's archival evaluations in the next chapter, because both chapters use archival evaluations from several cities in a cumulative way. Both chapters will help policymakers to appreciate the importance of using multiple data sets and theories of change, especially when unexpected findings emerge that cut against a common wisdom.

• How can we use historical evidence in evaluations? Historians traditionally have not done many evaluations, yet their techniques for mining data archives fit naturally with evaluators' efforts to resolve conflicts or assess theories about public programs. Historians do not generally design prospective, randomized trials of any intervention. Yet some of the most important policy questions, when framed as evaluation challenges, lend themselves beautifully to good archival analysis.

Jennifer Light's chapter accomplishes exactly this. It presents the results of archival evaluations and uses techniques of a historian to explore how an increasingly common withdrawal of wealthier citizens from certain societal engagement unexpectedly results in greater demand for public services. A substantial literature argues that "the secession of the successful" should result in more public services for everyone else. Light, who has written about the history of technology using archival evaluation, finds that the common wisdom is not quite right. She documents that in many cities, citizens who use private home security systems unexpectedly end up increasing their demands for public police services—demands that inevitably reduce public services available for less rich citizens.

The consistency of Light's findings across a variety of heterogeneous cities buttresses her argument that privatization of home security actually increases demands placed on public police. Her findings include evidence from areas as diverse as Beverly Hills, California; New York City; Houston; Dallas; Rochester, Minnesota; Multnomah County, Oregon; Riverside, California; and Blue Springs, Missouri. When any one city or county conducts an evaluation that turns up surprising results, those results might be dismissed as idiosyncratic. Yet when more than half a dozen sites find the same pattern, policymakers are forced to take notice. In the end, policymakers acknowledge that the consistency of such findings across many sites can begin to create a new common wisdom.

• Evaluators must develop more systematic ways to integrate findings about program effectiveness with data about program costs. For many years, evaluations across multiple fields focused on outcomes without much attention to costs. Evaluations that asked, "Does Head Start work?" and "Does WIC [the nutrition program for low-income pregnant women] work?" were the norm. Yet increasingly this question is inadequate, especially for policymakers. The chapters by Michael Stoto and Henry Levin illustrate this inadequacy. Each shows that attention to costs, using a version of cost-effectiveness analysis that should be familiar to many evaluators, resulted in recommendations to change existing public policies that at first seemed "obviously correct." Once again, good evidence led to change in a widely held common wisdom.

Stoto explores what evaluations reveal about the most effective strategy for preventing perinatal transmission of human immunodeficiency virus (HIV). Based on his work with a study panel at the Institute of Medicine, Stoto notes that the common wisdom among public health commissioners and epidemiologists was quite settled for many years. It was that targeting of prevention programs offers the best outcomes, especially when the distribution of the characteristic we want to prevent (HIV) is so remarkably heterogeneous. It is widely agreed that "the HIV infection rate is concentrated in women of color in the Northeast and South, especially in women who use drugs themselves or whose sexual partners do so."

Stoto presents evaluation findings based on cost-effectiveness analyses that dramatically changed prevention policies throughout the nation. He illustrates that a public policy of targeting, the common wisdom used until the late 1990s, was in fact less effective policy than adopting universal HIV testing with patient notification, as a routine component of prenatal care.

Stoto summarizes the epidemiological evidence that originally led to proposals for targeting. He then describes a multifaceted evaluation that came to exactly the opposite conclusion. The analysis takes geographic differences into account as part of its structure, thus including states with higher HIV rates (such as New York, New Jersey, and Florida), as well as many states with lower rates, to allow for comparisons. Stoto's powerful conclusion is that the best prevention strategy is "to target programs, and not people." This conclusion cut precisely against accepted wisdom in the public health community and changed prevention policies.

In Chapter Five, Henry Levin makes another compelling case for more cost-effectiveness analyses, especially in education. Levin argues that as a form of evaluation and policy analysis, cost-effectiveness may even serve as a threat to decision makers by providing information that is counter to common sense, popular appeal, and the traditional support of particular constituencies.

Levin's argument is that evaluations in education make astonishingly little use of this technique in contrast to, say, health policy evaluations. He documents this argument with specific evidence from an extensive literature search. Levin makes a compelling case that too many evaluators are ignoring a powerful method for comparing alternative policies that would give evaluators valuable guidance about their relative costs and results. The goal is to provide guidelines about which policy alternative provides the most impact relative to cost.

Levin illustrates his argument with a specific evaluation case study from California. He reports that a statewide effort to improve reading and math focused on three statewide interventions: a longer school day, smaller class size, and more computers in classrooms. The one finding from a high-quality evaluation that found peer tutoring to be the most cost-effective policy intervention cut against the common wisdom. Levin reports that in contrast to the surprising health finding that Stoto reported, this education result was considered so unexpected and surprising that it has been ignored for several years. Only now are educators considering its consequences.

• Evaluators read increasingly about the value of combining quantitative and qualitative evidence. Yet few examples offer compelling evidence that illustrate the concrete value of combining both to improve policy. More specific examples are needed. David Pillemer's chapter provides a superb example of combining different forms of evidence: data from state legislative policies and educational evaluations. Pillemer explores a growing concern among educators, students, and parents.

Twenty-six states have passed laws requiring that students in public schools pass a standards-based test before they can receive a high school diploma. Private sector corporations and state legislatures overwhelmingly support such standards-based testing, but parents and teachers often are less supportive. A common question that critics of sole reliance on standardized tests raise is, "How can we learn what types of teaching and learning processes contribute to successful performance in school?"

Pillemer describes a new kind of evaluation strategy, autobiographical memory research, that can help teachers and school leaders improve instruction. He does this in the context of mandated standardized testing, arguing that the two sets of data taken together are far more powerful than either format taken alone. New data analysis methods enable evaluators to go beyond case examples and harness more systematically the lessons contained in autobiographical reports.

Pillemer describes in detail the implementation of an evaluation technique that so well complements the widely known, traditional standardized tests that are increasingly mandated. He also offers several examples from interviews with college students that readers will quickly identify as having a special power. Underlying Pillemer's evaluation procedures is the empirical finding that students' remembering and describing certain classroom details is related to accurate test performance. Pillemer describes empirical evidence that this finding characterizes both high school and college students.

• Evaluations can benefit from stressing a careful examination of what treatment was actually implemented and whether the implemented treatment was the intended treatment. Edward Miech, Bill Nave, and Frederick Mosteller use three case studies that rely heavily on qualitative evidence and reach a fascinating and unexpected conclusion about the impact of professional development training for K–12 teachers. Their case studies carry a special strength since all three authors are distinguished statisticians who usually emphasize, and are known for, their quantitative analyses.

The analyses focus on three sites: New York City, Pittsburgh, Pennsylvania, and several sites in the Annenberg School professional development consortium. It is precisely the differences among these three sites that allow Miech, Nave, and Mosteller to draw their conclusions about unexpected findings for teacher development.

Their finding about the impact of professional development programs evaluated by the Annenberg Program is surprising. It turns out that after exposure to certain training, teachers claimed that their classroom behavior did not change. Yet outside observers repeatedly found exactly the opposite: changes in behavior despite teachers' belief that nothing was different.

This chapter raises the question of what constitutes compelling evidence for change: outside observers' findings from evaluations or self-reports of people whose judgment we generally trust and respect.

Taken together, these six chapters serve two great purposes. First, they offer six concrete examples of evaluation findings that cut against a common wisdom. In so doing, they offer policymakers a chance to change current practices based on evidence. Second, they offer specific examples of five profitable directions that scholars and practitioners can explore in future work. I view these chapters not as an end but rather as a great start. Each illustrates a productive next step that the field of evaluation can take to broaden and enrich its repertoire of tools and techniques, especially as we sometimes need to push against a common wisdom. These chapters give some good news: that it is often possible to dislodge a widely held common view, and even to change public policies, when well-designed evaluations turn up findings that may be unexpected but nonetheless are compelling.

RICHARD J. LIGHT is professor of education at the Harvard Graduate School of Education and the Kennedy School of Government. He is chair of the Changing Demographics in Colleges Project at the American Academy of Arts and Sciences.

2

In response to cumulative evaluation findings, police departments around the nation have changed the way they respond to calls dealing with domestic violence. Policies have been changed in response to evaluation evidence.

Evaluating Arrest for Intimate Partner Violence: Two Decades of Research and Reform

Rosemary Chalk, Joel H. Garner

Intimate partner violence (also termed domestic violence) is a serious social problem. Of the 3,419 cases of homicide that involved female victims in 1998, approximately one-third of these women were murdered by a spouse, ex-spouse, or boyfriend (Centers for Disease Control, 2000). Recent survey data suggest that approximately 1.5 million women were physically assaulted or raped by a current or former intimate partner in 1995–1996 (Tjaden and Thoennes, 1998). Other surveys suggest that the magnitude of the problem is much greater if threats such as stalking and physical harassment are included. Initial studies indicate that annual direct costs of medical care for battered women average about $1.8 billion (Miller, Cohen, and Rossman, 1993). Other estimates of national costs (which vary by criteria regarding inclusion of costs of medical care, treatment and prevention programs, and workplace and productivity costs) range from $5 billion to $67 billion (Chalk and King, 1998).

Despite the magnitude of victimization rates and service use costs, little certainty exists within the research community regarding the effectiveness of intimate partner violence treatment and prevention programs. In a comprehensive review of what is known about the effectiveness of treatment or prevention programs for all types of family violence (including child abuse and neglect and elder abuse, as well as intimate partner violence), the National Research Council (NRC) surveyed over two thousand studies published between 1980 and 1996 (Chalk and King, 1998). Of these studies, the NRC committee identified only thirty-four evaluations that involved an

NEW DIRECTIONS FOR EVALUATION, no. 90, Summer 2001   © Jossey-Bass, A Publishing Unit of John Wiley & Sons, Inc.

intervention designed to treat some aspect of domestic violence, used an experimental or quasi-experimental design, and measured and used violence as an outcome measure. The selected studies involved interventions that were distributed across different service settings: half (eighteen studies) involved legal interventions (such as arrest, prosecution, or judicial reforms); the remaining half were divided between seven studies that involved social service interventions (such as battered women's shelters) and nine studies that involved interventions in health care settings (such as curriculum changes or new emergency room protocols).

In this chapter, we consider the implications of findings that emerged from a subset of studies from the NRC review known as the police arrest studies. Much of the material discussed draws on previously published work developed by Joel Garner and Christopher Maxwell (2000).

History of the Police Arrest Studies

The initial study of the deterrent effects of police arrest for intimate partner violence was conducted in Minneapolis between 1981 and 1983 (Sherman and Berk, 1984a). This study, commonly known as the Minneapolis study, is one of the most visible and highly cited research articles in criminology (Cohn and Farrington, 1996). It was followed by a set of eight experimental police arrest studies in six sites initiated in 1985 and 1986, known collectively as the Spouse Assault Replication Program (SARP). All studies, funded by the U.S. Department of Justice, tested the deterrent effectiveness of the police making an arrest (or issuing an arrest warrant) for misdemeanor assaults against a spouse or intimate partner. Different research teams conducted each study in separate jurisdictions across the United States. The replication sites were Omaha, Nebraska; Milwaukee, Wisconsin; Charlotte, North Carolina; Colorado Springs, Colorado; and Dade County, Florida. A sixth replication police arrest study was funded and initiated by the Atlanta Police Department, but it has not published any findings or produced a final report as of 2000.

The initial study in Minneapolis, conducted by the Minneapolis Police Department (Sherman and Berk, 1984a, 1984b), represented a "sea change in the nature of criminological research" (Garner and Maxwell, 2000, p. 7). The proposal for the study called for a rigorous test of deterrence theory, using an experimental design to assess the deterrent effect of arrest on the crime of spouse assault. The study design addressed many methodological concerns that had been highlighted in an earlier criticism of criminological research on rehabilitation. These concerns included the use of nonequivalent control groups, no controls for variation in follow-up periods, and single measures of outcomes. The Minneapolis arrest study also represented a significant shift in criminological research by making victim safety, not police officer safety, the sole measure of success in evaluating the deterrent effects of arrest practices in response to spousal violence.

The Minneapolis study randomized three alternative responses to incidents of misdemeanor domestic violence: arrest, separation of the couple (also known as a "cooling-down" procedure, such as a walk around the block), or counseling. Data were collected from 314 experimental incidents, official police records of the subsequent criminal behavior of the suspects, and interviews with victims. The study was implemented in only two precincts in Minneapolis, and a small number of volunteer police officers participated in shaping the study design and implementation. A Minneapolis-based domestic violence coalition was also involved with the implementation of the study and became an important partner in publicizing the research results.

Sherman and Berk (1984a, 1984b) reported that the use of arrest reduced recidivism (measured by victim interviews, as well as police reports of subsequent intimate partner violence) by as much as 50 percent within the following six months. They reached this conclusion by comparing the rates of reoffending between the experimental and control groups. The recidivism rate for the arrest subjects was 14 percent, and the rate of suspects who were not arrested was 21 percent.

The findings of the Minneapolis study, concluding that arrest produced deterrence by achieving a 50 percent reduction in recidivism, were widely publicized. Subsequent publications included a Police Foundation report (Sherman and Berk, 1984a) and news stories in the Science section of the *New York Times* (Boffey, 1983), electronic and print media (Sherman and Cohn, 1989), and peer-reviewed scientific journals (Sherman and Berk, 1984b; Berk and Sherman, 1988).

The results of the Minneapolis study were quickly endorsed by the U.S. Attorney General's Task Force (1984), which urged police jurisdictions throughout the United States to adopt pro-arrest polices in addressing incidents of domestic violence. Many jurisdictions did so, in the expectation that they too would experience dramatic declines in recidivism rates.

The Importance of Replication Research

Despite the enthusiasm for the initial arrest study, early praise was tempered by recommendations that stressed the need to replicate this research. The original authors urged replication (Sherman and Berk, 1984b), as did the U.S. Attorney General's Task Force that had promoted implementation of the findings. National Institute of Justice (NIJ) officials, however, expressed concern about the expense of a replication effort, which threatened to consume a substantial portion of their modest research budget. Furthermore, serious objections were voiced about the political pitfalls that could result from a replication effort that might produce results differing from the initial results or could undermine future research investments by supporting politically unpopular responses to intimate partner violence.

Despite these reservations, NIJ decided to support the SARP studies. The research reports that emerged from the replication studies (Black, Berk,

Lilly, and Rikoski, 1991; Dunford, Huizinga, and Elliott, 1989; Hirschel and others, 1991; Pate, Hamilton, and Annan, 1991; and Sherman and others, 1991) generated new uncertainties and inconsistencies about the effectiveness of arrest as a deterrence to intimate partner assault.

Two major surprises emerged from the replication research studies. First, the initial round of studies did not substantiate the original finding that arrest produced a large deterrent effect by reducing future recidivism rates. Although interviews with victims in some study sites suggested that offenders were less likely to reoffend following an arrest incident, this effect could not be documented in official police records. These inconsistencies in the police arrest research literature led the NRC committee to conclude in 1998 that "arrest in all misdemeanor cases will not on average produce a discernible effect on recidivism" (Chalk and King, 1998, p. 176).

A second surprise occurred with the development of more sophisticated studies that allowed researchers to reanalyze original data and individual records from all six experimental sites associated with the police arrest research (Maxwell, 1998; Garner and Maxwell, 2000). That research has indicated that although insufficient evidence exists in the published police arrest studies to support the effectiveness of arrest as a deterrent to intimate partner violence, an independent multisite reanalysis of the original research data provides a more favorable assessment of the deterrent effects of research.

The Importance of Study Design, Definitions, Data, and Measures

The collective group of studies within the police arrest literature represented an attempt to improve the quality of criminological research by strengthening the design of research focused on an important social problem. Highly visible public debates over the value of criminal justice sanctions and deterrence as effective crime control strategies in the 1970s led to a study by the National Academy of Sciences (NAS) that stressed the importance of using experimental design in examining the relative merits of changes in levels of criminal sanctions (Blumstein, Cohen, and Nagin, 1978; Zimring, 1978).

Similar language appeared almost twenty years later in another National Academy of Sciences study on family violence prevention and treatment programs. The family violence study concluded:

> The urgency of the need to respond to the problem of family violence and the paucity of research to guide service interventions have created an environment in which insights from small-scale studies are often adopted into policy and professional practice without sufficient independent replication or reflection on their possible shortcomings. Rigorous evaluations of family violence interventions are confined, for the most part, to small or innovative programs that provide an opportunity to develop a comparison or control study, rather than focusing on the major existing family violence interventions.

This situation has fostered a series of trial-and-error experiences in which a promising intervention is later found to be problematic when employed with a broader and more varied population. . . . The programmatic and policy emphasis on single interventions as panaceas to the complex problems of family violence, and the lack of sufficient opportunity for learning more about the service interactions, client characteristics, and contextual factors that could affect the impact of different approaches, constitute formidable challenges to the improvement of the knowledge base and prevention and treatment interventions in this field [Chalk and King, 1998, p. 291].

Efforts to determine the actual effects of the original Minneapolis experiment and the interventions in the replication sites have included close readings of the original reports, attempts to reconstruct the archived data, a meta-analysis of the published data, and an independent multisite analysis of the unpublished research data, including individual records. Each new effort has provided useful insights into the points of agreement and inconsistency with the original findings, revealing diverse findings that result from methodological differences in study design, definitions, and data analysis. These methodological differences create noise in the evaluation literature that is a common practice in social research and leads to the identification of important factors that influence outcomes and analysis. But as Garner and Maxwell (2000) observe, the diversity in research findings from similar experiments can frustrate those policymakers who are trying to inform, if not base, policy on research findings.

Minneapolis Study. The original study in Minneapolis found a specific deterrent effect for arrest based on an analysis of 314 experimental cases that were randomly assigned to arrest, separation, or counseling interventions by the responding police officers. Randomization was controlled by police officers, not the research team. Sixteen cases (about 5 percent of the experimental cases) were excluded because "no treatment was applied or the case did not belong in the study (i.e., a fight between a father and son)" (Sherman and Berk, 1984a, p. 264). The investigators used an innovative technique to "correct" for the misapplication of treatments that has not been fully documented in their technical reports. But it is impossible from the published reports of the Minneapolis study to determine the extent to which the exclusion of sixteen experimental cases or the use of statistical corrections influenced the direction, size, and statistical significance of the original experiment (Garner and Maxwell, 2000).

In studying rates of recidivism, the Minneapolis research team relied on two sources that were both studied six months following the experimental incident: official police records and subsequent interviews with victims. In the victim interviews, violent acts and threats of violence were counted as failures (half of the reoffending instances involve threats only). The level of new violence reported in the victim interviews was about 26 percent.

In a secondary analysis of the data from the Minneapolis experiment, Gartin (1991) concluded that the central elements of the original analyses were reproducible, despite the fact that significant proportions of the original data were omitted in the archival data (Berk and Sherman, 1988). Gartin's analysis, conducted as part of a dissertation supervised by Sherman, generally confirmed the original findings, but indicated that the existence of statistically significant effects for arrest depended on the type of data source and the choice of analytical model. Gartin used a new data source, the analysis of police dispatch data, in combination with victim interviews and criminal history data. This new measure revealed no differences between arrest and other treatments, causing Gartin to report that the weight of the evidence "seems to indicate that there was not as much of a specific deterrent effect for arrest" (p. 16) as suggested by the original reports.

The decision to replicate the original study led to a series of negotiations over the extent to which replication studies must adhere to the study design. The replication effort was announced as a research study, not a demonstration project, but NIJ did not provide subsidies to the participating departments for the significant administrative burdens associated with participating in rigorous research studies.

Seventeen law enforcement agencies submitted proposals; six were selected for final support. NIJ required that each replication involve experimental comparisons of alternative policy responses to misdemeanor spouse assault incidents and measure victim safety using both official police records and victim interviews (National Institute of Justice, 1985). But the replication research teams and police agencies were able to select other elements of the study design. Several other sites implemented more than one experiment.

Omaha Study. Omaha implemented the first SARP study and conducted two police arrest experiments in 1986 and 1989. The two experiments are commonly described as offender-present and offender-absent. The first experiment (offender-present) was a close replica of the Minneapolis study, including random assignment of arrest, separation, and counseling in misdemeanor intimate partner violence incidents (Dunford, Huizinga, and Elliott, 1990). The offender-present study offered methodological improvements: the researcher, not a police officer, controlled randomization, and a high proportion of victims were interviewed. The offender-present study also used a more restrictive definition of new violence, with reoffending limited to actual violence with injury to the victim and excluding threats of violence.

In the second experiment (offender-absent), conducted simultaneously with the first, an arrest warrant was randomly assigned in incidents when the offender was not present when the police arrived (Dunford, 1990). The arrest warrant intervention was a novel response to the finding that offenders were absent more than 40 percent of the time when police arrived on the scene and found probable cause to make an arrest. Dunford reported that warrants were consistently associated with lower reoffending rates, and on several of their measures, the differences were statistically significant.

Following a common data collection and analysis approach developed by NIJ, both experiments in Omaha reported the prevalence, frequency, and time to first new offense, in addition to the prevalence rate analysis used in the original Minneapolis reports. (Berk and Sherman, 1988, used similar data in a reanalysis of the original data and continued to report statistically significant deterrent effects.) The approaches to data collection and analysis were part of a general recommendation for criminological research that had been made by a 1986 NAS report for future research on criminal careers (Blumstein, Cohen, Roth, and Visher, 1986).

In general, the findings of the Omaha offender-present experiment did not confirm the original Minneapolis study. Even with the more restrictive condition of subsequent violence, Dunford and his colleagues reported that arrested offenders were more likely to reoffend based on official police records and less likely to reoffend based on victim interviews. However, none of these findings was large enough to be statistically significant, leading to a final conclusion that arrest "neither helped nor hurt victims in terms of subsequent conflict" (Dunford, Huizinga, and Elliott, 1990, p. 204). They also observed that both official records and victim interviews indicated the occurrence of multiple new offenses. The total number of offenses was higher for arrested suspects than for suspects not arrested, but neither of these effects was statistically significant. In their time-to-failure analysis, deterrence appeared to produce positive effects in victim interviews (longer time intervals) but opposite effects in official records, yet here again the findings were not statistically significant. The implication was that arrest could decrease the proportion of suspects with new offenses but increase the total number of new offenses against a smaller number of victims (Garner and Maxwell, 2000).

Charlotte Experiment. Studies by Hirschel and his colleagues (Hirschel, Hutchinson, and Dean, 1992; Hirschel and Hutchison, 1992) in Charlotte, North Carolina, compared three police actions—custody arrest, citation, and advising—and used victim interviews and police records to examine recidivism rates. The results from the Charlotte study were similar to those reported in Omaha: official record data indicated that arrest was associated with increased reoffending rates, while victim interviews indicated that arrest reduced reoffending rates. Yet neither effect was statistically significant, causing the investigators to report that their experiment provided no evidence of a deterrent effect from arrest.

Milwaukee Experiment. The studies in Minneapolis, Omaha, and Charlotte were all conducted in relatively small geographic areas with limited sample sizes; Minneapolis had 330 experimental incidents, Omaha had a combined total of 577 incidents in two experimental studies, and Charlotte had 652 incidents. The Milwaukee study was the first to use a sample size and randomization pattern that were sufficiently large to determine medium and even small effects in addition to large effect sizes. Over twelve hundred experimental cases were recorded in the study, including interviews with 921 victims (Sherman and others, 1991, 1992; Sherman, 1992).

The results of the Milwaukee experiment were consistent with those reported in Omaha and Charlotte: no statistically significant reductions in recidivism rates for arrested suspects were reported in official records or in victim interviews. In fact, the opposite trend was found: arrested suspects had higher rates of reoffending in both official records and victim interviews, undermining the notion that arrest deters subsequent violence.

The Milwaukee study did introduce several novel features designed to test other forms of deterrence. Subjects who were arrested were assigned arbitrarily to short or long periods of incarceration, but no difference occurred between the two arrest treatments.

A third source of data collection for reoffenses was added to the Milwaukee study: records of police calls to the local shelter. This measure also indicated higher rates of reoffending for the arrested subjects, with a difference that was statistically significant (Sherman and others, 1991).

Dade County Experiment. Two experiments were implemented in Dade County, which covers much of the metropolitan area of Miami, Florida. The first involved a replication of the Minneapolis experiment with just two treatments: arrest and no arrest. The second experiment used the same incidents as the first but randomly assigned half the cases to an existing program of follow-up services in Dade County. These services were designed to provide more options to victims in addressing violent relationships, assuming that additional resources would assist victims in avoiding abusive partners in the future or participating more actively in their prosecution.

The victim interviews in the first Dade County experiment found that arrest reduced future offending; the results were statistically significant. The official records also showed arrest to be associated with decreased reoffending, but the effect was not statistically significant (Pate, Hamilton, and Annan, 1991). The victim interview results were the first confirmation of the effects observed in Minneapolis and increased the likelihood that arrest had a deterrent effect for intimate partner violence.

In addition, the analysis of the participation of victims in follow-up services indicated no differences in future recidivism rates as measured by either official records or victim interviews. The study team concluded that the statistical power of this experiment supported a conclusion that follow-up services did not protect the victims of intimate partner violence, but their results were not published. Garner and Maxwell (2000) observe that this important finding on the limited ability of follow-up services has been consistently omitted from the subsequent review literature on police arrest studies.

Colorado Springs Experiment. The Colorado Spring Police Department conducted the largest SARP study, consisting of 1,660 experimental incidents (Black, Berk, Lilly, and Rikoski, 1991; Berk, Campbell, Klap, and Western, 1992a). The cases were assigned to four treatment groups: arrest, separation, on-scene counseling, and postincident counseling. This experiment reported results comparable to those of Dade County. A deterrent effect of statistical significance was found using the rate of reoffenses from the victim interviews, but the deterrent effect found in official records was not statistically significant. The effect sizes were judged to be credible because of the size of the data collection effort; the study team interviewed 84 percent of the victims (1,350 victims) at least once, for a total of 6,032 interviews. Interviews were conducted both shortly after the experimental incident and about six months afterward. The study team also attempted to interview three-fourths of the victims by telephone on a biweekly schedule for up to three months. The extensive interviewing raises questions about the amount of attention and surveillance introduced in the study design, which could contribute to or detract from the safety of the victims (Garner and Maxwell, 2000). Results based on the Colorado Springs victim interviews have recently been published (Maxwell, 1998).

Qualitative and Quantitative Approaches to Research Syntheses

In a recent review and analysis of the police arrest research literature, Garner and Maxwell (2000) offer several reflections on the merits of prior assessments:

• *Qualitative judgments may not be adequate to discern small or medium effects of selected interventions when weighing and integrating a large body of evidence from diverse studies.* Garner and Maxwell take exception to the conclusion of the NAS study on family violence that indicated that arrest will not "produce a discernible effect on misdemeanor spouse assault" (Chalk and King, 1998, p. 176). The NAS study emphasized that no large effects associated with arrest had been consistently reported in the police arrest research studies, but the study committee did not offer specific criteria for defining a "discernible" effect. Because their review was limited to the information available in the published literature, the NAS committee did not have an opportunity to conduct a secondary analysis of original data that might reduce the uncertainty associated with the research base.

• *The customary practice of simply counting the number of studies supporting or not supporting a specific hypothesis can produce inaccurate estimates because it overlooks the strength of selected effects and sample size.* In reviewing the findings of the different experimental sites, Garner and Maxwell (2000) note that it is inappropriate to assume that each jurisdiction has a single and easily identified finding for or against deterrence. This method assumes that studies with 330 incidents are equivalent to those with 1,600 incidents and that a single study with a large deterrent effect is equivalent to one study with a small escalation effect (and vice versa). Counting studies represents an improvement over more imprecise qualitative approaches in synthesizing and assessing research literature, but it lacks the evidentiary strength associated with more systematic and quantitative efforts to summarize the overall effect of a body of research.

• *Analytic techniques designed to compute a standardized effect size across multiple studies show much promise, but this approach requires consideration of the impact of moderator variables.* In reviewing the police arrest research literature, Sugarman and McCoy (2000) observe that controlling for different moderator variables can contribute to variation in effect sizes and suggest ways to reduce heterogeneity by constructing a data set of effect sizes. They indicate that this approach is especially useful for guiding policy formation when research literature yields inconsistent results or conflicting findings. In analyzing the data from the six experimental sites, Sugarman and McCoy (2000) conclude that arrest policies have no overall main effect on recidivism when police arrest reports are used to assess recidivism. A different data source, victim interviews, shows that police arrests did reduce violence recidivism significantly more than mediation and separation interventions, but this finding may be influenced by selection in who agrees to be interviewed. Violence that does not include specific injury or incidents (such as threats) may show up only in the victim interviews. These authors also conclude that the variation among the effect sizes can be accounted for by chance, and therefore the effect sizes do replicate each other. But the overall effect size is small: a 5.2 percent decrease in recidivism associated with the arrest intervention. This meta-analytic review of data, focused on effect sizes, produces very different conclusions from narrative reviews or analyses that consider only p values and the direction of effects.

• *Secondary analyses of multisite studies offer valuable opportunities to introduce a common analytic approach, consistent definitions, and common measures and to consider new data elements that may have been overlooked in the initial analyses.* NIJ's long-standing policy of requiring the archiving of original research data has resulted in improved understanding of several controversial issues in criminology. A reanalysis of Erhlich's findings (1973) about the deterrent effects of criminal sanctions in a report by the NAS (Blumstein, Cohen, and Nagin, 1978) confirmed the original work but suggested that the results were dependent on the specifications of his econometric models. Blumstein, Cohen, and Gooding (1983) identified numerous data quality and data analysis limitations in research by Carlson, Evans, and Flanagan (1980) on the influence of prison cell space on future prison populations. Visher's reanalysis (1986) of Greenwood and Abrahamse's (1982) recidivism prediction scale demonstrated the extent to which alternative analytical approaches would generate less powerful results.

Numerous reanalyses of the data from the police arrest studies have now been conducted. These efforts include work by the original investigators (Sherman, 1992; Berk, Campbell, Klap, and Western, 1992; Pate and

Hamilton, 1992), as well as research by independent scholars (Maxwell, 1998; Garner and Maxwell, 2000). The reanalyses by Sherman (1992), Berk, Campbell, Klap, and Western (1992), and Pate and Hamilton (1991), using just official records of recidivism, conclude that the effect of arrest was dependent on a defendant's stakes in conformity such as marriage and employment. Maxwell (1998) and Garner and Maxwell (2000) use both official records and victim interviews and report that arrest does have a modest deterrent effect for offenses by males against their female intimate partners.

None of these secondary analyses would have been possible without the effort needed to document fully the original data and the placement and documentation of the data in a public archive. The importance of full documentation for understanding the effectiveness of arrest is reinforced by the fact that not all of the data from the original Minneapolis study have been saved and cannot be included in secondary analyses.

Where Do We Go from Here?

The experience with inconsistent and surprising findings in the police arrest studies yields several clues about the nature of the challenges, as well as important opportunities that have emerged in family violence research evaluations.

The challenges are formidable. First, sample sizes of family violence interventions must be large enough to reveal any significant effects as they occur. Introducing variations in the dependent variable (in this case, arrest, counseling, and separation) requires a sample size of well over one thousand experimental incidents. David Cordray and others have written about the importance of constructing samples that are large enough to have sufficient statistical power to reveal medium and small effects, as well as large results (see, for example, Cordray, 1986, 1993; Chalk and King, 1998). Creating large samples requires sustained time and effort and often depends on the interplay of multiple services and offices in a community setting, many of which have competing missions and different levels of resources.

Second, the evaluation of community-based interventions, especially changes in legal procedures or police actions, requires the full cooperation of administrative offices that may include police agencies, prosecutorial offices, and even judicial representatives. These offices must be willing to assume administrative burdens designed to benefit the research design rather than improve their own routine or current practice. In some cases, law enforcement agencies and others may need to have direct control over the process of randomization to protect principles of justice or fairness in the community. In the police arrest studies, key community figures in each of the study sites played important roles in the design and implementation of the research. These figures commonly included police chiefs who were committed to the improvement of law enforcement procedures and believed that research was a valuable tool in this effort. But the turnover in community leadership is a critical factor that can quickly undermine a promising research design when collaborative partners disappear from important positions of authority.

Third, promising results in one community require time and patience to determine their strength and limitations prior to implementation on a regional or national scale. The findings of the original Minneapolis study were broadly publicized and triggered a pro-arrest policy throughout the country, even while the study sponsor and others were considering the importance of a replication effort. Policymakers at the local, state, and national levels are often desperate for simple solutions to complex social problems, and the tendency to respond quickly to new findings is accelerating in this age of instantaneous communication and electronic access to new research. Unraveling sources of technical error, hidden bias, and weak statistical techniques requires additional time and effort that are too often uncompensated, and discouraged, especially at times when it is more important to get it first than to get it right.

Despite these challenges, several important opportunities have emerged in the wake of the police arrest literature. First, communities across the United States are increasingly aware that well-designed evaluation studies offer valuable ways to improve policy and practice, and ultimately to reduce costs, in addressing intimate partner violence. Many experimental initiatives were launched in the past few decades as part of a national pattern of social reform to prevent and control violence among intimate partners. State and federal agencies are now sifting through the array of activity to identify interventions that show promise of achieving significant results in controlling offenders, protecting victims, and preventing future incidents of violence. Congress has increased funds for research in this area, and new practice and research partnerships are emerging in many communities.

Next, researchers have acquired greater appreciation for the importance of developing multiple data sets and theories of change when examining complex social behaviors. The police arrest studies demonstrated that official records alone are often not sufficient to document changing norms and behaviors at the individual or group level. Interviews with victims have provided important opportunities to understand more about the dynamics, sequence, and intensity of intimate partner violence. These insights in turn are shaping theory and the design of new research instruments and methods. Multiple sources of data allow investigators to study trends and directions in research areas where the data are too weak or too fragmented to acquire sufficient statistical power to demonstrate strong associations and causality. Their development thus provides important building blocks in the evolution of new research fields.

Finally, the police arrest research literature provides an important archival record that can support other research studies on related but different phenomena. One new topic emerging in studies of intimate partner violence, for example, is the effect of adult-to-adult violence on children. By reviewing the case reports that were documented as part of the police arrest studies, Fantuzzo, Boruch, Beriama, and Marcus (1997) have learned more about the role that children play as triggers, witnesses, and mediators of violence in their homes. This important field of study will undoubtedly bring its own surprises in the wake of future evaluations of yet-to-be-designed interventions. By building rich data sets that can inform multiple experimental studies and hypotheses, the police arrest studies have formed a research foundation that stands as a valuable model and framework for the entire field of research on violence.

References

Berk R. A., Campbell, A., Klap, R., and Western, B. "Bayesian Analysis of the Colorado Springs Spouse Assault Experiment." *Journal of Criminal Law and Criminology,* 1992, *83,* 170–200.

Berk, R. A., and Sherman, L. W. "Police Responses to Family Violence Incidences: An Analysis of an Experimental Design with Incomplete Randomization." *Journal of the American Statistical Association,* 1988, *83,* 70–76.

Black, H., Berk, R. A., Lilly, J., and Rikoski, G. *Evaluating Alternative Police Response to Spouse Assault in Colorado Springs: An Enhanced Replication of the Minneapolis Experiment, 1987–1989. Final Report.* Colorado Springs: Colorado Springs Police Department, 1991.

Blumstein, A., Cohen, J., and Gooding, W. "Capacity on Prison Population: A Critical Review of Some Recent Evidence." *Crime and Delinquency,* 1983, *29,* 1–51.

Blumstein, A., Cohen, J., and Nagin, D. (eds.). *Deterrence and Incapacitation: Estimating the Effects of Criminal Sanctions on Crime Rates.* Washington, D.C.: National Academy Press, 1978.

Blumstein, A., Cohen, J., Roth, J., and Visher, C. (eds.). *Criminal Careers and "Career Criminals."* Washington, D.C.: National Academy Press, 1986.

Boffey, P. "Domestic Violence: Study Favors Arrest." *New York Times,* Apr. 5, 1983, p. C1.

Carlson, K., Evans, P., and J Flanagan, J. *American Prisons and Jails.* Vol. 2: *Population Trends and Projections.* Washington, D.C.: National Institute of Justice, 1980.

Centers for Disease Control and Prevention. "Building Data Systems for Monitoring and Responding to Violence Against Women: Recommendations from a Workshop." *MMWR,* 2000, *49*(RR-11), 1.

Chalk, R., and King, P. (eds.). *Violence in Families: Assessing Prevention and Treatment Programs.* Washington, D.C.: National Academy Press, 1998.

Cohn, E., and Farrington, D. "Crime and Justice and the Criminal Justice and Criminology Literature." In D. Sherman (ed.), *Crime and Justice: A Review of Research, 20.* Chicago: University of Chicago Press, 1996.

Cordray, D. S. "Quasi-Experimental Analysis: A Mixture of Methods and Judgment." In W.M.K. Trochim (ed.), *Advances in Quasi-Experimental Design and Analysis.* New Directions for Program Evaluation, no. 31. San Francisco: Jossey-Bass, 1986.

Cordray, D. S. "Synthesizing Evidence and Practice." *Evaluation Practice,* 1993, *14*(1), 1–8.

Dunford, F. W. "System-Initiated Warrants for Suspects of Misdemeanor Domestic Assault: A Pilot Study." *Justice Quarterly,* 1990, *7*(4), 631–653.

Dunford, F. W., Huizinga, D., and Elliott, D. S. *The Omaha Domestic Violence Police Experiment. Final Report.* Washington, D.C.: National Institute of Justice, U.S. Department of Justice, 1989.

Dunford, F. W., Huizinga, D., and Elliott, D. S. "The Role of Arrest in Domestic Assault: The Omaha Police Experiment." *Criminology,* 1990, *28*(2), 183–206.

Ehrlich, I. "Participation in Illegitimate Activities: A Theoretical and Empirical Investigation." *Journal of Political Economy,* 1973, *81*(3), 521–565.

Fantuzzo, J. W., Boruch, R., Beriama, P., and Marcus, L. "Domestic Violence and Children: Prevalence and Risk in Five Major U.S. Cities." *Journal of the American Academy of Child and Adolescent Psychiatry,* 1997, *36*(1), 116–122.

Garner, J. H., and Maxwell, C. D. "What Are the Lessons of the Police Arrest Studies?" In S. K. Ward and D. Finkelhor (eds.), *Program Evaluation and Family Violence Research.* New York: Haworth Press, 2000.

Gartin, P. R. *The Individual Effects of Arrest in Domestic Violence Cases: A Reanalysis of the Minneapolis Domestic Violence Experiment. Final Report.* Washington, D.C.: National Institute of Justice, 1991.

Greenwood, P. A., and Abrahamse, A. *Selective Incapacitation.* Washington, D.C.: National Institute of Justice, 1982.

Hirschel, J. D., and Hutchison, I. W. "Female Spouse Abuse and the Police Response: The Charlotte, North Carolina, Experiment." *Journal of Criminal Law and Criminology,* 1992, *83*(1), 73–119.

Hirschel, J. D., Hutchison, I. W., and Dean, C. W. "The Failure of Arrest to Deter Spouse Abuse." *Journal of Research in Crime and Delinquency,* 1992, *29,* 7–33.

Hirschel, J. D., and others. *Charlotte Spouse Assault Replication Project. Final Report.* Washington, D.C.: National Institute of Justice, 1991.

Maxwell, C. "The Specific Deterrent Effect of Arrest on Aggression Between Intimates and Spouses." Unpublished doctoral dissertation, Rutgers University, 1998.

Miller, T. R., Cohen, M. A., and Rossman, S. B. "Victim Costs of Violent Crime and Resulting Injuries." *Health Affairs,* 1993, *12,* 186–197.

National Institute of Justice. *Replicating an Experiment in Specific Deterrence: Alternative Police Responses to Spouse Assault.* Washington, D.C.: National Institute of Justice, 1985.

Pate, A., Hamilton, E., and Annan, S. *Metro-Dade Spouse Assault Replication Project: Draft Final Report.* Washington, D.C.: Police Foundation, 1991.

Sherman, L. W. *Policing Domestic Violence: Experiments and Dilemmas.* New York: Free Press, 1992.

Sherman, L. W., and Berk, R. A. *The Minneapolis Domestic Violence Experiment.* Washington, D.C.: Police Foundation, 1984a.

Sherman, L. W., and Berk, R. A. "The Specific Deterrent Effects of Arrest for Domestic Assault." *American Sociological Review,* 1984b, *49,* 261–272.

Sherman, L. W., and Cohn, E. G. "The Impact of Research on Legal Policy: The Minneapolis Domestic Violence Experiment." *Law and Society Review,* 1989, *23*(1), 117–144.

Sherman, L. W., and others. "From Initial Deterrence to Long-Term Escalation: Short Custody Arrest for Poverty Ghetto Domestic Violence." *Criminology,* 1991, *29*(4), 821–850.

Sherman, L. W., and others. "Crime, Punishment, and Stake in Conformity: Legal and Informal Control of Domestic Violence." *American Sociological Review,* 1992, *57,* 680–690.

Sugarman, D. B., and Boney-McCoy, S. "The Art of Reviewing Research." In S. K. Ward and D. Finkelhor (eds.), *Program Evaluation and Family Violence Research.* New York: Haworth Press, 2000.

Tjaden, P., and Thoennes, N. *Prevalence, Incidence, and Consequences of Violence Against Women: Findings from the National Violence Against Women Survey—Research in Brief.* Washington, D.C.: National Institute of Justice and Centers for Disease Control and Prevention, 1998.

U.S. Attorney General. *Attorney General's Task Force on Family Violence.* Washington, D.C.: U.S. Government Printing Office, 1984.

Visher, C. "The RAND Inmate Survey: A Reanalysis." In A. Blumstein, J. Cohen, J. Roth, and C. Visher (eds.), *Criminal Careers and "Career Criminals."* Washington, D.C.: National Academy Press, 1986.

Zimring, F. "Policy Experiments in General Deterrence." In A. Blumstein, J. Cohen, and D. Nagin (eds.), *Deterrence and Incapacitation: Estimating the Effects of Criminal Sanctions on Crime Rates.* Washington, D.C.: National Academy Press, 1978.

ROSEMARY CHALK is senior research associate at Child Trends Inc. and a former study director at the Institute of Medicine.

JOEL H. GARNER is director of research at the Joint Centers for Justice Studies.

3

Archival analyses reveal how privatization increases rather than decreases public spending.

The Effects of Privatization on Public Services: A Historical Evaluation Approach

Jennifer S. Light

What is the evidence about the impact of privatization on public resources? Using home security systems as a case study and historical evaluation as a method, I reexamine the assumption that the growth of a private security industry has reduced demands of wealthier citizens on public police and the public purse. Evaluation evidence based on historical research casts serious doubt on whether the apparent creation of a parallel, private system is in fact resulting in reduced demand for public services.

The sections that follow illustrate how observers who view private security in opposition to public police do not account for areas like alarm response, where the private and public sectors have a cooperative, if ambivalent, relationship (Cunningham and Taylor, 1985). Security devices may symbolize privatization and withdrawal, yet alarm users' demand for service from public police in fact remains high. Thus, while privatization is described as a "retreat of the state" (Swann, 1988), evaluation evidence in this case reveals that the state does not retreat. The case of alarms offers a vivid account of the unexpected consequences of privatization.

This article has five sections. Section One presents the common wisdom on privatization from a prominent group of social observers. I call their perspectives "fortress narratives." Section Two cross-examines these fortress narratives. Evaluation questions from the history of technology help us to assess critically their claims about social change and begin the search for contrary evidence. Section Three uncovers several contradictions in the privatization of security. I juxtapose fortress narratives with new information from historical sources to reveal a surprising mismatch between the consequences of privatization that these interpretations anticipate and the actual consequences documented by historical data. The argument that Americans are buying out of the common life in their choices for crime prevention can be turned on its head when reexamined in the light of this evidence. This close evaluation study of a single technology raises a set of broad questions for scholars and policymakers confronting policy challenges posed by privatization. In Section Four, I suggest how discrepancies between privatization in theory and in practice suggest the need for a different kind of conversation about privatization. This new conversation would place the growth of private security technologies and services, and their relation to the allocation of public policy resources, more prominently on a public policy agenda. Finally, the Conclusion calls for a serious national discussion grounded in empirical data to clarify relationships between public policy and the private security industry.

The Common Wisdom

An entirely parallel, private system exists to provide schools, playgrounds, parks, and police protection for those who can pay, leaving the poor and less well-to-do dependent on the ever-reduced services of city and county governments. . . . In areas where citizens feel let down by local government, it is not surprising that those who can afford to turn to private service provision do [Blakely and Snyder, 1997a, p. 95].

A prominent group of American social observers has expressed urgent concern about the collective consequences of privatization. In articles and books with titles like "Secession of the Successful," *The Revolt of the Elites, Democracy's Discontent,* and *Fortress America,* social critics such as Robert Reich, Christopher Lasch, Michael Sandel, Edward Blakely, and Mary Gail Snyder cast critical eyes on privatization as a source of growing social inequality (Blakely and Snyder, 1997a, 1997b; Davis, 1990; Ellin, 1997; Flusty, 1994; Lasch, 1995; McKenzie, 1994; Reich, 1991; Sandel, 1996; Spitzer, 1987). Privatization has multiple meanings, and these observers emphasize three: privatization as the search for privacy—the loss of community; privatization as a constriction of public space—the privatization of the public sphere; and, most notably, privatization as a replacement of public services and community institutions with market alternatives—the creation of a parallel private system. In schooling, housing, health care, and policing, private options seem to present the affluent with a total retreat from the common life, with public and community institutions left to serve only the poor. As a result, both these institutions and American civil society are depleted.

Among the phenomena these commentaries treat is the growth of a private security industry. Private security officers patrolling U.S. residential neighborhoods and businesses have outnumbered public police since the early 1970s (Shearing, 1992; Kakalik and Wildhorn, 1972; Cunningham and Taylor, 1985; Cunningham, 1990). Today a remarkable one-fifth of homes in the United States are equipped with electronic security systems (Pedersen-Pietersen, 1997). In these critical readings, private police and self-protective gadgetry represent a "fortressing" of America, transforming security from a social good produced through the informal surveillance of neighbors' eyes on the street into a commodity that sets people apart. As affluent citizens choose private protection, Americans with fewer financial resources are left with bad service from poorly funded public police. Only a sustained national conversation about revitalizing community and renewing social obligation can begin to repair what these observers identify as the problems of privatization.

Three Evaluation Questions

> The carefully manicured lawns of the Westside [of Los Angeles] spread ominous little signs threatening "ARMED RESPONSE!" Wealthier neighborhoods in the canyons in Hillside scour behind walls guarded by gun-toting private police and state-of-the-art electronic surveillance systems. . . . This militarization of city life is increasingly visible everywhere in the built environment of the 1990s [Davis, 1992, p. 154].

Critics who investigate the collective social consequences of privatization make many compelling observations about contemporary life:

* Economic divisions are increasing.
* Rich and poor citizens have unequal access to security.
* Fear of crime is often out of proportion to actual victimization risk.
* Private security systems and services ironically may create fear in order to reduce it.
* Privatized public spaces and services have important implications for civic life.

So what could be wrong with these conventional interpretations?

Evaluation using historical research is well suited to question common wisdom. Both the skepticism historians bring to accounts of social change over time and the open-ended nature of historical and archival research lend themselves to allow for unexpected findings. I begin the search for contrary evidence by cross-examining existing research, using three basic questions that historians of technology often ask. It is important to understand that when historians of technology use the word *technology,* we refer not only to individual devices but also to techniques (such as urban planning) and systems (such as the electrical grid).

* *Does the argument make claims about the role of a technology in social progress or its role in cultural decline?* One of the most frequently repeated stories about technology tells how a given device or technological system

has served as an engine of positive or negative social change (Douglas, 1986; Fischer, 1992; Marvin, 1987; Rheingold, 1993). A common variant is that technology connects us, or separates us, linking observations about technology to an issue that has captured American interest since de Tocqueville: the tension between individualism and isolation versus community and civic engagement (Adorno, 1934, quoted in Levin, 1990; Hayden, 1984; Lynd and Lynd, 1956; Oldenburg, 1989; Postman, 1992; Putnam, 1996; Slater, 1970; Sorkin, 1992). These themes reappear and intersect in fortress narratives, which characterize home security systems as technological extensions of wealthy citizens' desire for isolation and exclusion.

Historians who study the social dimensions of technological change learn quickly to become skeptical about accounts of a technology's role in such unidirectional social change. Technologies are complex artifacts and are not independent of the society in which they are created (Bijker, Hughes, and Pinch, 1987; MacKenzie and Wacjman, 1985;). A device's array of interactions with different individuals and groups makes it difficult for any particular technology to have monolithic or predictable effects (Fischer, 1992; Wajcman, 1991). The reappearance of such stock stories here, explaining home security technology as exemplifying the decline of community and civil society, presents a first clue that the situation may be more complicated. Any claims of technology's universal social effects—positive or negative—deserve scrutiny, suggesting the need to look for evidence that may cut in another direction.

Contemporary critics recognize that the desire for security, and unequal protection, is not new. Wealthy citizens have long fenced their property and hired doormen or guards. Private policing predates state responsibility for police service, as the title of Les Johnston's *The Rebirth of Private Policing* (1991) reminds us. What these critics suggest is new, and sinister, about privatizing security is privatization itself. We might then look for evidence showing that much of what is considered fortressing in fact results from a more democratic society, where a wider variety of citizens now believe that they have a right to walk down the streets of more affluent neighborhoods. Such free movement was not an option in earlier periods. According to this view, it is not because of an increasing segregation of society but precisely because it is much more integrated that alarm systems have become so common. What electronic alarms allow is a more open, public face to the world.

• *Does the argument's characterization of a technology look at how that technology is used?* In their focus on isolation and the decline of civil society, narratives about "fortress America" fall into the interpretive category that Raymond Williams (1975) calls "symptomatic approaches." These approaches read technologies as expressing a prevailing view of society; here we find that observers see home security systems alongside privatization's catchall list of developments with important social and political effects. Yet as an interpretive genre, symptomatic approaches often reveal less about a technology and more about the staying power of "characteristic modes of explanation" (Schudson, 1984, p. 135) as scholars invest objects with meanings independent of any actual use. Designers' and even users' intentions for technology, while a vivid record of individual hopes, do not accurately predict or portray the actual effects of a device's use over time.

Home security systems encompass an array of options. For example, security monitoring may originate from a local police switchboard or a national center several states away. Private security services may or may not have branch offices with alarm runners near a subscriber's home. That people may act as central components in making technological systems function (Hughes, 1983) is an important detail here, for home security systems depend on a network including technology, the private security industry, neighbors, and public police. To what extent do these different permutations have the same effects?

The stories we tell about technology are only as good as the evidence we gather, and research in the history of technology suggests that evaluators must look at the use of a technology within a broad context and over time to understand its effects. Short-term modes of thinking risk overlooking the long-term contradictions that some technologies generate (Fischer, 1992; Forrester, 1969; Slater, 1970; Tenner, 1996). A technology's effects may differ by user group or place of use. Other technologies of the same era may exert opposing effects (Fischer, 1992). And people may welcome one aspect of a technology while resisting another. These possibilities suggest that further research about use is needed to assess whether and to what extent different kinds of private security systems share common effects.

• *What are they really talking about?* This question flows directly from the most basic evaluation question that historians bring to any set of sources: Who are the authors? How authors explain change over time, and whether they construct this change as problematic, often reveals more about how they see society than about any specific empirical social reality (Gusfield, 1981; Schudson, 1984). According to this view, evaluators must pay careful attention to whether observations about phenomena such as the privatization of security are in fact political arguments about something else.

Looking at fortress narratives' observations about technology in the light of the first two evaluation questions, it becomes increasingly clear that security technology itself is not so central to the argument about the collective consequences of privatization. In fact, private security is rarely the singular focus in these jeremiads, but rather is presented as merely one example of a broader phenomenon that includes the privatization of schools, public space, media, health care, and housing. Both of these observations offer clues suggesting that criticisms of privatized security are less commentaries on the security industry and more commentaries on what these observers believe has gone wrong with American society.

At the heart of most fortress narratives is a negative interpretation of the impact of reduced social services and worries about consequences that accompany an increased role for the market. These trends are said to have effects on security, citizenship, and, ultimately, democracy. According to this view, civic life has been corrupted by the market as a preoccupation with individual "rights," including individuals' right to spend, has superseded social obligation, and the only practice of citizenship is through the market (Lasch, 1995; Glendon, 1991). Such observations are extensions of the critique of American individualism leveled by de Tocqueville (1956), who wrote that individualism, expressed through isolation, might lead to the downfall of public life. Understanding how private security serves as a placeholder for a broader argument about the commodification of American life, important questions emerge. Do the consequences of privatization in institutions from schooling to media to policing follow the same predictable path? Where is it possible to find concrete data that really tell us about how privatization works?

Each of the three questions suggests new directions for evaluation based on gathering additional evidence. A rich stock of data on home security systems across the past three decades is contained in the written record. Mainstream newspapers and magazines, specialist publications such as *Police Chief,* think tank reports on the alarm industry from the RAND and Hallcrest Corporation, local municipal codes from Illinois to Hawaii, police data on alarm response, and archival records of home security equipment testing at Consumers' Research Incorporated provide the foundation for my alternative evaluation here of the effects of home security systems.

Contradictions emerge between widely accepted narratives about home security technology and the ways its actual implementation and use affect peoples' lives. By focusing on alarms' technical details, the demands that alarms place on public police, and how existing public policies treat the devices, none of which figures prominently in fortress narratives, I consider how, in constructing fortress America as a problem of privatization, these accounts ignore other important consequences.

The Findings That Surprise

Too often, alarm users and the alarm industry expect the police to be merely an extension of an electronic security system functioning as a piece of equipment [Holcomb, 1977, p. 68].

There are important reasons to be concerned about the effects of the home security systems used in an estimated 20 percent of American households. Yet these are not the same reasons suggested by accounts of privatization and the fortressing of America. My research on the use of home security technology since the late 1960s has uncovered some contradictions in the privatization of security. The argument that affluent citizens are buying out of the common life can be turned on its head to reveal some surprising consequences when we remember three details about alarm use.

First, home security systems, which encompass a range of devices, are not merely the province of wealthy Americans. Archival records of pricing from Consumers' Research Incorporated Archives and more recent issues of publications such as *Consumer Reports* reveal devices priced for a broad middle class of consumers, as well as a large group of alarm hobbyists (Consumers' Research Incorporated Archives; "Alert," 1990; "Burglar Alarms," 1994; "Home Security Test," 1998; Gorman, 1979). Second, on account of their origins in military sensor technology, systems of all types are highly prone to malfunction: an astonishing 95 percent of alarm activations are false alarms, unchanged over the past three decades. Third, while the private purchase of home security technology may suggest an intention to "fortress," in practice it is public police who must ultimately respond to these apparently privatized forms of security. This police time is paid for by all taxpayers, rich and poor (Daughtry, 1993; Kleinknecht and George, 1988; Sweeney, 1983).

- *A first surprise: The number of police hours spent responding to alarms is high.* As more Americans have purchased home security systems, the number of police hours spent responding to false alarms has increased. The consequences for police of this high false alarm rate have been astounding, and an array of findings in the historical evaluation literature quantify these consequences. Six examples illustrate:

In Beverly Hills, California, a survey of the last three months of 1970 revealed that 99.4 percent of the over 1,000 alarm calls to which police responded were false alarms (Kakalik and Wildhorn, 1977).

In 1981, the New York City Police Department responded to 400,000 alarm calls, of which 98 percent were false. This took up 15 percent of radio car runs in that city (Cunningham and Taylor, 1985).

In 1982, the Houston Police Department responded to 78,562 false alarms, billing 15 percent of police time at a cost of $7 million (Cunningham and Taylor, 1985).

In 1992, Dallas police estimated their annual cost of servicing false alarms at $6.3 million: "Answering those 147,010 calls [one-fifth of all calls to police] occupied the equivalent of 80 full-time police officers working the whole year" (Jacobson, 1993, p. 1A). Dallas's police department organized an entire alarm unit to deal with this task.

According to 1996 data, low crime and high alarm use created conditions whereby "in some neighborhoods, almost half of all police calls were to check burglar alarms," including 117 responses to calls from a single address (Bartels, 1996, p. 4A).

In the 1990s, police across the United States responded to more than 13.7 million alarms per year, at a 98 percent false alarm rate (Blackstone and Hakim, 1996).

Accounts of fortress America emphasize the irony that security devices increase fear among some users. (Trade publications from the 1970s at the Consumers' Research Incorporated Archive are filled with industry discussions of how to create fear in order to sell consumers on security technology.) Perhaps more ironic is that excessive false positives subverted a central motivation for purchasing an alarm in the first place. As early as 1971, police reported great frustration:

> In responding to these alarms, police expend valuable resources which could be better utilized elsewhere. Police officer alertness and interest may become dulled after investigating repeated false alarms. Officers and citizens are subjected to the threat of traffic accidents during fast vehicular response to false alarms. Or, as is done in some cities, police may reduce the priority of alarm responses and in busy periods may arrive too late to apprehend the burglar [Kakalik and Wildhorn, 1977, p. 417].

An early requirement that "an alarm means at least two police units responding at emergency speeds" did not characterize the situation for long (Holcomb, 1977, p. 68). Police cars speeding to an apparent crime scene posed potential public hazards. In the case of false alarms, ten to twenty minutes spent checking a house for intruders took time away from responding to actual crimes in progress.

• *A second surprise: The trend toward remote monitoring has not resulted in a "revolt of the elites against the constraints of time and place" (Lasch, 1995); rather, it has resulted in increased calls for service from public police.* In the 1970s, when alarm ownership was at only 2 percent (Greer, 1991) and many systems connected directly to police switchboards, growth in ownership alongside persistent false alarms catalyzed debates about privatizing alarm response. Historical sources document a vigorous debate about the advantages and disadvantages of hiring private companies that lack police powers. Police relished pointing out why they were better and more effective than the private companies, although in many cases they were unwilling providers of residential security services. (Compare, for example, Boughton, 1976; Cunningham and Taylor, 1985; Gordon, 1988; Gribbin, 1972; Holcomb, 1977; Metias, n.d.; "Electronic Alarms," 1973; Usher, 1992; Zethraus, 1998).

Replacing direct connections to police with central station services, a trend in the 1970s and 1980s, did not resolve the problem. The theoretical model of privatization as increasing efficiency, or at the very least reducing the drain on police resources through intervention, did not work well in practice. Crime is a local phenomenon, so as one guide observed, a national service might not provide the best protection: "Hooking a silent alarm into a security service is not cheap, and unless the security service has an office nearby it may be an exercise in futility. Being connected to a service where the agents have to drive twenty miles to answer an alarm isn't going to catch many burglars" (Keogh and Koster, 1977, p. 99).

Police saved some time because such arrangements provided some "false-alarm screening, especially during storms. Besides, they eliminate the often frustrating police hunt for someone to reset the sounding alarm" (Gribben, 1972, p. 9). Yet central stations located in other states demanded local police response if a household could not confirm a signal was false. Even companies that sent local alarm runners or private security officers to reset alarms would often simultaneously call in police backup.

Historical evidence reveals how cooperation between local police and private security organizations has played a critical role in the home security system. The public-private partnership undergirding this system assumed greater importance as technological developments made remote monitoring increasingly common (Greer, 1991). With reductions in the cost of long-distance lines and the development of two-way communications, regional and even national private monitoring centers emerged in the 1980s. The first such super-central station, the National Alarm Computer Center (NACC), in Irvine, California, opened in 1978. The NACC contracts with multiple alarm companies and is the largest monitoring facility in the United States. It is not unusual now for an emergency call to be routed through another state, and Kornheiser (1998) describes the frustrations of a Maryland homeowner whose alarm signal is routed through Kansas City.

Private monitoring operating from such a distant station has had to contact alarm subscribers' local police if an alarm was triggered. Without police following up such calls, the technological sophistication of a private service has not guaranteed protection beyond a deterrent effect. The most expensive services might dispatch armed alarm runners or private security officers to hold suspects, but these agents need police to make the final arrest. Indeed, the suggestion that private companies operate a parallel private system overlooks an important fact: private security officers' power of arrest. With only a few exceptions, a private security officer employed by Guardsmark or Westec has the same power of arrest as any other private citizen or neighborhood patrol. Hiring private officers does not eliminate the ultimate need for police backup as the final step in the public-private system. Thus, the use of private security was in essence a contract with public police for increased service. Privatization in theory is turned on its head in actual practice.

• *A third surprise: Local ordinances regulate private devices to support continuing police response, yet they do so without compelling evidence that such ordinances achieve their goals.* Depictions of a parallel private system ignore the places where private actions and public policies intersect. As partial privatization of alarm services did not significantly reduce burdens on public police, local officials turned to alarm ordinances as a way to recoup some of the public costs. Across the United States, an array of local ordinances increasingly undertook to regulate the use of private devices—both the minority still directly connected to police and the majority monitored by private companies. These include permits for alarm use, fees for false alarms that summon police, and a variety of licensing standards and rules for alarm businesses and private security officers. Geographical variation among both technologies and ordinances complicates any simple story of alarms' effects. Yet one constant is the role that local government plays in controlling the use of these devices and related services.

Individual municipalities have taken different positions as to whether alarm monitoring should be a public or private responsibility. Most categorize police responses to alarms actually triggered by intruders as a public service. Yet they classify response to false alarms as a private service, since it detracted from other police duties (Longmont, Colorado, 1993). Ordinances passed across the country articulated this distinction as they wrote costs into law. In some areas, with the authority of municipal code behind them, police have met overactive systems and unpaid fines with the penalty of low-priority response, nonresponse, or permit revocation.

For example, in the 1970s, an ordinance in Englewood, New Jersey (where police still offered direct services), allowed owners three false positives per year. This was followed by a fifteen-dollar fine, then a twenty-five-dollar fine, and finally, at the sixth fine, the alarm would be disconnected from the police board (Phalon, 1973). Los Angeles City Council's 1973 alarm ordinance revoked permits after four false alarms within any four-week period (Shepard, 1977). In South Polk County, Florida, an ordinance from 1997 grants permit holders two "free" false alarms. The third false alarm nets a fifty-dollar fine, increasing each time by twenty-five dollars, to a maximum of five hundred dollars (Samoliski, 1998). In Rochester, Minnesota, an ordinance specifically discussing "Failure to Pay Assessments" explains how "police may reduce the priority of the police response to Alarm Dispatch Requests at their Alarm Site until such payment has been made" (Rochester, Minnesota, 1997).

These fines and threats achieved the desired results in some places, yet overall results were mixed. In Multnomah County, Oregon, a false alarm ordinance from 1975 reduced false alarms by 47.3 percent by 1977 (Watts, 1977). In contrast, Dallas's permit system, in effect since 1982, seemed ineffective given that in 1995, "Police studies show that half of all false alarms originate from unregistered systems. In other words, police spend a lot of time responding to alarms that are in violation of a city ordinance" ("False Alarms," 1995, p. 22A).

Idiosyncratic differences across municipalities illustrate how local politicians iteratively retooled local regulations to accommodate them rather than ban malfunctioning alarms. For example, in Missouri, the Blue Springs Police grandfathered subscribers already connected to the police department but, beginning in 1992, forced new customers to find private alternatives (Blue Springs, Missouri, 1992). Such was the cooperative, if ambivalent, relationship between public and private sectors.

In some sense, many calls for service to public police—to rescue a cat, to send an ambulance—are private uses of public resources. What is distinct about alarms is that a majority of alarm calls are false positives. Police have found themselves in a catch-22: servicing false alarms wastes police time, yet the opposite response—inaction—can have dire consequences. In 1992 in Riverside, California, a woman was raped and beaten in her home. The intruder set off her alarm, but police did not respond because she had not paid the permit fee ("Cops Ignore Alarm," 1992). Riverside rescinded its nonresponse policy, although similar laws remain in city codes and municipal ordinances in many communities across the United States. This extreme incident highlights the challenge that private alarm use poses to public police. Although 95 to 98 percent of activations might be false, what about the 3 to 5 percent of alarms actually triggered by intruders?

Consequences of the Evaluation Findings

With more than 3 million burglaries around the country every year resulting in losses exceeding $2 billion, you'd expect the police to be falling all over themselves to praise burglar-alarm systems. But ask patrol officers about their value as a crime prevention tool and the clamor or abuse is likely to be deafening [Sharpe, 1981, p. 1].

The archival evaluation offered here reveals how questions and methods from the history of technology can usefully inform contemporary policy debates. Fortress narratives' claims about community and democracy in decline, or the "secession of the successful," may perhaps characterize America today. Yet in the case of security, we see from historical evaluations that such claims, linked to privatization, oversimplify complex institutional relationships between private and public sector groups, highly influenced by the limitations of alarm technologies. While fortress accounts favor a national conversation about privatization that emphasizes renewing civic obligation, the findings presented here suggest instead that we begin a conversation that reevaluates current policies guiding the provision of public police services to alarm owners.

The Law Enforcement Assistance Administration, a now-defunct federal agency, briefly launched the private security industry and the topic of alarm use into the public eye in the 1970s, a time when public police were just beginning to comprehend the scope of the burgeoning industry and its potential impact. At that time, only 2 percent of residences had outfitted themselves with security systems (Greer, 1991). Central monitoring services were far more likely to be located near subscribers' homes. Consequences for law enforcement of a high false-alarm rate were real, but far less significant than with the current 20 percent usage rate and a standard of remote monitoring.

The consequences of private individuals' choices to continue using devices that malfunction so often demand further study. Ultimately the technological imperfections shift costs to the public sector. There is no reason to think that individual households and consumers will change their behavior if current public policies persist. Alarm permits and occasional fines for overexcitable alarms are small prices to pay for access to essentially private services from public police. In the case of private schools, there may be redistributive financial benefits to public bodies when families pay taxes for public services they are not using. But policing differs from schooling because reliance on its private counterpart does not negate reliance on the public version. If the cost to society of an individual household's choice to maintain a security system does not reflect a more accurate accounting of police response to false alarms, as well as the lost access to police services for others, then individuals who choose private systems will continue their substantial call on public resources.

Conclusion

Problems posed by alarm technologies, alongside the enormous growth of a private security industry, offer public police another opportunity to reevaluate the services they now provide. A serious national discussion grounded in empirical data would do much to clarify relationships between public police and the private security industry. The most extreme consequence of such a reevaluation would be a call for total privatization of some services like alarm response. Yet realistically, policy decisions are unlikely to be homogeneous or national, since individual neighborhoods continue to have different law enforcement needs.

For example, in cities, where the majority of crimes take place, inequalities resulting from the use of alarms are most readily apparent. Police response to false alarms in middle-class and affluent urban neighborhoods reduces police presence in areas experiencing more violent crime. By contrast, in affluent suburbs, where public law enforcement serves a more homogeneous population, police may encourage the use of alarms in the absence of other pressing service needs. In these areas, a call for service that is a false alarm is less likely to draw resources away from other populations.

How, given local differences, do we evaluate core public services that police must offer, and which should be privatized? If contracting out implies that only those who can afford to pay for certain kinds of protection get that service, then at what level should society fund police so that they offer similar services to those who cannot afford it? These questions have been part of vigorous policy debates about privatization in schooling and health care. Yet they are hard to find on the agenda in public policy discussions of policing.

The language of fortress America, and its reference to broad issues of social justice, remains a powerful rhetorical strategy to describe emerging forms of social inequality. Yet fortress accounts ignore empirical evaluation data attesting to how the inefficiencies of privatization exert their effects. In the case of home security systems, these inefficiencies have created an unexpected form of inequality: home security devices have become a significant constituent of how police spend their time, and local public policies support a significant allocation of resources by police to service these imperfect technological devices.

The case of home security offers a compelling example of the value of historical evaluation research for contemporary public policy. Historical methods make it possible to process a massive amount of data from a broad set of sources, picking up examples that run counter to accepted interpretations. The unexpected gap between privatization in theory and in implementation identified here raises practical issues for policymakers confronting privatization beyond security. As we seek to balance public needs and fairness with the collective consequences of privatization, further historical evaluations will deepen our understanding of this complex phenomenon.

References

"Alert: How to Choose an Alarm System." *Consumer Reports,* 1990, *55*(2), 104.

Bartels, L. "Time's About Up for False Alarms: Council Clears Plan to Register Home Security System, Deter Calls." *Rocky Mountain News,* Sept. 6, 1996, p. 4A.

Bijker, W., Hughes, T., and Pinch, T. (eds.). *The Social Construction of Technological Systems.* Cambridge, Mass.: MIT Press, 1987.

Blackstone, E., and Hakim, S."Crying Wolf with Public Safety." *American City and County,* 1996, *111,* 54.

Blakely, E., and Snyder, M. G. "Divided We Fall: Gated and Walled Communities in the United States." In N. Ellin (ed.), *Architecture of Fear.* New York: Princeton Architectural Press, 1997a.

Blakely, E., and Snyder, M. G. *Fortress America.* Washington, D.C.: Brookings Institution Press, 1997b.

Blue Springs, Missouri. Municipal Code 210.060. 1992.

Boughton, P. "Do You Need a Burglar Alarm?" *Consumer Gazette,* Dec.–Jan. 1976, p. 30.

"Burglar Alarms: Defense Against Intruders." *Consumer Reports,* 1994, *59*(5), 329.

"Cops Ignore Alarm; Woman Raped." *Chicago Tribune,* Mar. 27, 1992, p. 10D.

Cunningham, W. *Private Security Trends: 1970–2000, The Hallcrest Report Two.* Boston: Butterworth-Heinneman, 1990.

Cunningham, W., and Taylor, T. *Crime and Protection in America: A Study of Private Security and Law Enforcement Resources and Relationships, Executive Summary from the Hallcrest Report.* Washington, D.C.: U.S. Government Printing Office, 1985.

Daughtry, S. "False Alarm Reduction: A Priority for Law Enforcement." *Police Chief,* Jan. 1993, p. 14.

Davis, M. *City of Quartz.* London: Verso, 1990.

Davis, M. "Fortress Los Angeles: The Militarization of Urban Space." In M. Sorkin (ed.), *Variations on a Theme Park: The New American City and the End of Public Space.* New York: Hill and Wang, 1992.

Douglas, S. "Amateur Operators and American Broadcasting: Shaping the Future of Radio." In J. Corn (ed.), *Imagining Tomorrow: History, Technology, and the American Future.* Cambridge, Mass.: MIT Press, 1986.

"Electronic Alarms: Let the Buyer Beware." *Business Week,* July 21, 1973, p. 84.

Ellin, N. (ed.). *Architecture of Fear.* New York: Princeton Architectural Press, 1997.

"False Alarms: Dallas Devises New Ways to Fight the Problem." *Dallas Morning News,* Dec. 12, 1995, p. 22A.

Fischer, C. *America Calling: A Social History of the Telephone to 1940.* Berkeley: University of California Press, 1992.

Flusty, S. *Building Paranoia: The Proliferation of Interdictory Space and the Erosion of Spatial Justice.* West Hollywood, Calif.: Los Angeles Forum for Architecture and Urban Design, 1994.

Forrester, J. *Urban Dynamics.* Cambridge, Mass.: MIT Press, 1969.

Glendon, M. A. *Rights Talk: The Impoverishment of Political Discourse.* New York: Free Press, 1991.

Gordon, D. "Home Security Systems, Alarming Trend, Private Security Companies' Popularity Grows as Police Response Times Rise." *Los Angeles Times,* July 12, 1988, p. K1.

Gorman, B. "Burglar Alarms: Not-So-Silent Sentries for Your Home." *Consumers Digest,* July-Aug. 1979, p. 26.

Greer, W. *A History of Alarm Security.* Washington, D.C.: National Burglar and Fire Alarm Association, 1991.

Gribben, A. "Those Fancy Home Burglar Alarms Turn Off Police." *National Observer,* Oct. 21, 1972, p. 9.

Gusfield, J. R. *The Culture of Public Problems: Drinking-Driving and the Symbolic Order.* Chicago: University of Chicago Press, 1981.

Hayden, D. *Redesigning the American Dream: The Future of Housing, Work and Family Life.* New York: Norton, 1984.

Holcomb, R. "Burglar and Hold-up Alarm Systems: An Overview." *Police Chief,* June 1977, pp. 66–69.

"Home Security Test." *Consumer Reports,* 1998, *63*(9), 54.

Hughes, T. *Networks of Power: Electrification in Western Society, 1880–1930.* Baltimore, Md.: Johns Hopkins University Press, 1983.

Jacobson, S. "Cause for Alarm: City Officials Say Home Security Devices' False Alerts Costing Taxpayers Millions." *Dallas Morning News,* Mar. 14, 1993, p. 1A.

Johnston, L. *The Rebirth of Private Policing.* London: Routledge, 1991.

Kakalik, J. S., and Kakalik, S. *Private Police in the United States: Findings and Recommendations.* Washington, D.C.: U.S. Government Printing Office, 1972.

Kakalik, J. S., and Wildhorn, S. *The Private Police: Security and Danger.* New York: Crane Russak, 1977.

Keogh, J. E., and Koster, J. *Burglarproof: A Complete Guide to Home Security.* New York: McGraw-Hill, 1977.

Kleinknecht, G. H., and George, D. A. "False Alarms: A Drain on Police Resources." *FBI Law Enforcement Bulletin,* Jan. 1988, p. 12.

Kornheiser, T. "Alarming But True." *Washington Post,* July 5, 1998, p. F1.

Lasch, C. *The Revolt of the Elites and the Betrayal of Democracy.* New York: Norton, 1995.

Levin, T. "For the Record: Adorno on Music in the Age of Its Technological Reproducibility." *October,* 1990, *55,* 23–66.

Longmont, Colorado. Municipal Code 6.98.010. Private Alarm Systems, "Declaration of Policy." Ord. 0–92–29 sec. 1. Amended During Recodification. 1993

Lynd, R., and Lynd, H. *Middletown: A Study in American Culture.* Orlando, Fla.: Harcourt Brace, 1956.

MacKenzie, D., and Wacjman, J. *The Social Shaping of Technology: How the Refrigerator Got Its Hum.* Milton Keynes, U.K.: Open University Press, 1985.

Marvin, C. *When Old Technologies Were New.* New York: Oxford University Press, 1987.

McKenzie, E. *Privatopia.* New Haven, Conn.: Yale University Press, 1994.

Metias, G. *Report of the Second Year of Operation-Installation and Evaluation of a Large-Scale Burglar Alarm System for a Municipal Police Department.* Cedar Rapids, Iowa: Police Department, n.d.

Oldenburg, R. *The Great Good Place: Cafes, Coffee Shops, Community Centers, Beauty Parlors, General Stores, Bars, Hangouts, and How They Get You Through the Day.* New York: Paragon House, 1989.

Pedersen-Pietersen, L. "Betting on Security as Crime Takes a Holiday." *New York Times,* May 11, 1997, p. 5.

Phalon, R. "Home Burglar Alarms Vex the Police." *New York Times,* Aug. 13, 1973, p. 33.

Postman, N. *Technopoly: The Surrender of Culture to Technology.* New York: Knopf, 1992.

Putnam, R. "The Strange Disappearance of Civic America." *American Prospect,* 1996, 24. [http://epn.org/prospect/24/24putn.html].

Reich, R. "Secession of the Successful." *New York Times Magazine,* Jan. 20, 1991, p. 42.

Rheingold, H. *The Virtual Community: Homesteading on the Electronic Frontier.* Reading, Mass.: Addison-Wesley, 1993.

Rochester, Minnesota. Municipal Code 57.14, Failure to Pay Assessments. 1997.

Samoliski, C. "Too Many False Alarms Will Be Worthy of Fine." *Tampa Tribune,* Apr. 4, 1998.

Sandel, M. *Democracy's Discontent: America in Search of a Public Philosophy.* Cambridge, Mass.: Harvard University Press, 1996.

Schudson, M. *Advertising, the Uneasy Persuasion: Its Dubious Impact on American Society.* New York: Basic Books, 1984.

Sharpe, I. "A Hard Look: A Pain to Police: Burglar Alarms." *San Francisco Examiner and Chronicle,* Mar. 15, 1981, p. 1.

Shearing, C. "The Relation Between Public and Private Policing." In M. Tonry and N. Morris (eds.), *Modern Policing. Crime and Justice: A Review of Research.* Chicago: University of Chicago Press, 1992.

Shepard, D. "A Systems Approach for the Reduction of False Burglary and Robbery Alarms." *Police Chief,* June 1977, pp. 75–76.

Slater, P. *The Pursuit of Loneliness: American Culture at the Breaking Point.* Boston: Beacon Press, 1970.

Sorkin, M. (ed.). *Variations on a Theme Park: The New American City and the End of Public Space.* New York: Hill and Wang, 1992.

Spitzer, S. "Security and Control in Capitalist Societies." In J. Lowman, R. Menzies, and T. S. Palys (eds.), *Transcarceration: Essays in the Sociology of Social Control.* Aldershot, U.K.: Gower, 1987.

Swann, D. *The Retreat of the State: Deregulation and Privatisation in the UK and US.* New York: Harvester Wheatsheaf, 1988.

Sweeney, P. "The True Cost of False Alarms." *Police Magazine,* May 1983, p. 47.

Tenner, E. *Why Things Bite Back: Technology and the Revenge of Unintended Consequences.* New York: Knopf, 1996.

de Tocqueville, A. *Democracy in America.* New York: Signet, 1956.

Usher, J. "Privatization in Criminal Justice: One Perspective in Southern California." In G. W. Bowman, S. Hakim, and P. Seidenstat (eds.), *Privatizing the United States Justice System: Police, Adjudication, and Correction Services from the Private Sector.* London: McFarland Publishers, 1992.

Wajcman, J. *Feminism Confronts Technology.* Cambridge, U.K.: Polity Press, 1991.

Watts, S. "Multnomah County's False Alarm Research." *Police Chief,* June 1977, p. 70.

Williams, R. *Television, Technology, and Cultural Form.* New York: Schocken, 1975.

Zethraus, L. "UP Moves Toward Direct Monitoring for Home Security." *Dallas Morning News,* July 15, 1998, p. 1N.

JENNIFER S. LIGHT is assistant professor of communication studies and sociology and faculty fellow at the Institute for Policy Research, Northwestern University. She holds a doctorate in history of science from Harvard University.

4

This chapter presents evaluation findings based on cost-effectiveness analyses that dramatically changed perinatal HIV prevention policies across the nation.

Preventing Perinatal Transmission of HIV: Target Programs, Not People

Michael A. Stoto

In February 1994, the *New England Journal of Medicine* published results from the AIDS Clinical Trials Group protocol number 76 (ACTG 076) showing that the rate of transmission of human immunodeficiency virus (HIV) from infected mothers to their children could be reduced by about two-thirds (Connor and others, 1994). Given that as many as one out of three children born to HIV-infected mothers were infected themselves, these results represented a major breakthrough in the battle against AIDS. The distribution of HIV infection in women and children in the United States at this time was, and continues to be, remarkably heterogeneous. The epidemic was concentrated in women of color in the Northeast and South, especially in women who use drugs or whose sexual partners do so (Institute of Medicine, 1999).

Faced with these epidemiological facts, specialists in public health and preventive medicine naturally came to the conclusion that prevention

The project on which this chapter is based was requested by the U.S. Congress; the Department of Health and Human Services provided financial support. Members of the Committee on Perinatal Transmission of HIV include Marie McCormick (chair), Harvard School of Public Health, Boston; Ezra C. Davidson, Jr. (vice chair); Charles R. Drew, University of Medicine and Science, Los Angeles; Fred Battaglia, University of Colorado Health Sciences Center, Aurora; Ronald Brookmeyer, Johns Hopkins School of Public Health, Baltimore, Maryland; Deborah Cotton, Boston University Medical Center; Susan Cu-Uvin, Miriam Hospital, Brown University, Providence, Rhode Island; Nancy Kass, Johns Hopkins School of Public Health, Baltimore, Maryland; Patricia King, Georgetown University Law Center, Washington, D.C.; Lorraine Klerman, University of Alabama at Birmingham; Katherine Ruiz de Luzuriaga, University of Massachusetts Medical School, Worcester; Ellen Mangione, Colorado Department of Public Health, Denver; Stephen Thomas, Rollins School of Public Health, Emory University, Atlanta, Georgia; and Sten Vermund, University of Alabama at Birmingham. Members of the Institute of Medicine staff include Michael A. Stoto and Donna A. Almario.

programs—efforts to identify women who are infected and offer them appropriate therapy—should be targeted to the women most at risk. Indeed, while national policy statements issued after the ACTG 076 findings were published spoke about the utility of testing all women in prenatal care for HIV and treating those who tested positive, most policies were pointedly voluntary, and women who seemed at higher risk for HIV infection—as defined by race and ethnicity, socioeconomic status, association with intravenous drug use, or geography—were in fact more likely to be tested for HIV in prenatal care. An evaluation of these efforts by the Institute of Medicine (IOM), however, found that this targeted approach, which seemed so natural to epidemiologists, was indeed *not* the most appropriate policy for preventing perinatal transmission of HIV in the United States. Rather, it was recommended that the United States adopt a policy of universal HIV testing, with patient notification, as a routine component of prenatal care (IOM, 1999).

In order to clarify these surprising results, this chapter describes the epidemiologic evidence that suggests a targeted approach to prevention and then summarizes the IOM's multifaceted evaluation that led to the opposite conclusion. The IOM conclusions were based on surveys of prenatal care providers and interviews with affected women, on process and outcome evaluations, and on ethical and cost-effectiveness analyses. Much of this chapter is drawn directly from the IOM report (1999).

The Case for a Targeted Approach

In 1997, women accounted for 21 percent of AIDS cases in adults, and the proportion of all cases that are among females continues to grow. At least two-thirds of AIDS in women can be attributed to injection drug use either directly or through sex with drug users. Although a subset of women with HIV have injected drugs or have had sex with a known injection drug user, an increasing proportion of women have become infected through sexual activity with men whose risk behaviors were unknown to them. AIDS is more prevalent in African American and Hispanic women, in women in the Northeast and the South, and in women in large cities (Centers for Disease Control, 1997b; Wortley and Fleming, 1997).

Approximately six thousand to seven thousand HIV-infected women give birth every year. Trend data show a relatively steady national rate of HIV prevalence in childbearing women between 1989 and 1994, the last year for which data are available. There are, however, regional differences. In the Northeast, the epidemic of AIDS in women started and peaked earlier, and the number of childbearing women with HIV infection declined by 25 percent between 1990 and 1994. In the South, the epidemic started later, and there was a 25 percent increase in childbearing women with HIV between 1980 and 1991. In the latest national estimate, the prevalence of HIV in childbearing women was 17 per 10,000 (Davis and others, 1995).

Perinatal transmission accounted for at least 432 AIDS cases in the United States in 1997. Pediatric AIDS cases are concentrated in eastern states, especially in the New York metropolitan area. In 1996, three states alone—New York, New Jersey, and Florida—reported 330 cases. This represents 49 percent of the diagnosed cases, although only 15 percent of children are born in those states (Centers for Disease Control, 1996; Ventura, Martin, Curtin, and Mathews, 1998). In contrast to the concentration of perinatal AIDS cases in the Northeast, they are far less common in most geographical areas. In 1997, thirty-nine states had fewer than ten perinatally transmitted AIDS cases (Centers for Disease Control, 1997a).

HIV Infection in Pregnant Women and Newborns. Perinatal transmission can occur antepartum (during pregnancy), intrapartum (during labor and delivery), and postpartum (after birth), but most mother-to-infant transmission appears to occur intrapartum. The ACTG 076 protocol showed that a regimen of zidovudine (AZT) could reduce perinatal transmission to 8 percent in some populations (Connor and others, 1994), and subsequent studies have suggested that rates of 5 percent or lower are possible with aggressive antiretroviral therapy and other interventions such as elective cesarean section (International Perinatal HIV Group, 1999). To maximize prevention efforts, therefore, women must be identified as HIV infected as early as possible during pregnancy. Early diagnosis allows the mother to institute effective antiretroviral therapy for her own health. This treatment is also capable of significantly reducing perinatal transmission. HIV-infected pregnant women can also be referred to appropriate psychological, social, legal, and substance abuse services. Babies born to HIV-positive mothers can be started on AZT within hours of birth, as in the ACTG 076 regimen. In addition, mothers who know they are HIV positive can be counseled not to breast-feed their infants.

Policy Development. The ACTG 076 results quickly led the U.S. Public Health Service (PHS) to develop guidelines about counseling and testing of pregnant women for HIV infection (Centers for Disease Control, 1995). The guidelines called for counseling all pregnant women about the risk of AIDS, the benefits of HIV testing, and voluntary testing. The approach was endorsed by the American College of Obstetricians and Gynecologists, the American Academy of Pediatrics, and other professional groups. The essence of the PHS guidelines also has been adopted by most states, by either policy or legislation. Medical practice has changed in line with these recommendations, with an increasing proportion of women tested for HIV during prenatal care. As a result of these and other changes, there has been a substantial reduction—approximately 43 percent from a peak in 1992 to 1996—in the number of newborns diagnosed with AIDS (Centers for Disease Control, 1997b). (Data published after the IOM study suggest an even greater decline in subsequent years.) A reduction of this magnitude in only a few years represents great progress, yet it is far less than the ACTG 076 findings can offer.

Efforts to Prevent Perinatal Transmission of HIV

Two years after the publication of the ACTG 076 findings, Congress addressed perinatal transmission issues in the Ryan White Comprehensive AIDS Resources Emergency (CARE) Act Amendments of 1996 (Public Law 104–146). In addition to setting an interim national policy on these issues, the law called on the IOM to "conduct an evaluation of the extent to which State efforts have been effective in reducing the perinatal transmission of the human immunodeficiency virus, and an analysis of the existing barriers to the further reduction in such transmission."

The IOM interpreted the phrase "State efforts" in the congressional charge to include all efforts by public health officials and prenatal care providers in the states to implement the PHS guidelines in clinical care. To help guide its evaluation, the IOM found it helpful to consider the following chain of factors affecting perinatal transmission. Transmission depends on the proportion of women

- Who are infected with HIV
- Who become pregnant
- Who do not seek prenatal care
- Who are not offered HIV testing
- Who refuse HIV testing
- Who are not offered the ACTG 076 regimen
- Who refuse the ACTG 076 regimen
- Who do not complete the ACTG 076 regimen
- Whose child is infected despite treatment

Although this is not a perfect linearly schema, it did help the IOM committee focus its efforts. And although evaluation data were not available on each of these factors individually, the schema was valuable in determining what should be considered. In particular, the committee was able to find the following evidence bearing on the efficacy of existing programs. Much of the information comes from surveys undertaken by the states in response to the call for evaluation implicit in the Ryan White CARE Act Amendments of 1996. The following summary illustrates the findings of evaluation studies in at least thirty-one states.

Women Receiving Prenatal Care. In general, the United States has made great progress in reducing the number of women who receive no prenatal care. Down from more than 30 percent only a few decades ago, in 1996 only 4.2 percent of women received no prenatal care (National Center for Health Statistics, 1997). Many subgroups in the population, however, do not fare as well. Almost 12 percent of African American women who live in urban areas receive no prenatal care. In Manhattan, where perinatal transmission of HIV is highly prevalent, 22.1 percent of women receive no prenatal care (U.S. Department of Health and Human Services, 1992). Prenatal care is also a problem in the populations most affected with HIV. In the Center for Disease Control's (CDC) State Enhanced Pediatric HIV Surveillance Program (STEP) study of HIV-infected women in New Jersey, South Carolina, Michigan, and Louisiana, for instance, 14 percent received no prenatal care. In the same study, 35 percent of women who also used drugs received no prenatal care (Centers for Disease Control, 1998). Lack of prenatal care is thus an important factor in the nation's ability to prevent perinatal transmission of HIV.

Counseling and Offering HIV Tests. Evaluation studies carried out by the states showed that providers are generally aware of the ACTG 076 results, the PHS guidelines, and state testing laws. In Montana, for instance, 87 percent of providers in 1996 were aware of CDC recommendations (Montana Department of Public Health and Health Services, 1996). In the same year, 92 percent of providers in Michigan were aware of state HIV laws (Michigan Department of Community Health, 1997). According to a 1995 study in North Carolina, 90 percent of providers had heard of ACTG 076 results (Newton and Bell, 1997). In California in 1995, however, only 75 percent of obstetricians reported being familiar with the state HIV testing law (Segal, 1996). Awareness of the perinatal transmission prevention issues seems to be relatively high overall.

Provider practices, however, do not seem to reflect this awareness. For instance, 63 percent of providers in Oregon in 1997 reported encouraging all women to be tested (Rosenberg and others, n.d.). In Virginia in 1996, 54 percent of practices reported offering HIV tests to 76 to 100 percent of their patients (Riley, 1998). In Michigan in 1996, only 55 percent of obstetricians reported that they comply with the state law for routine HIV testing (Michigan Department of Community Health, 1997) (presumably this is an overestimate, because some providers may not be willing to report that they do not follow the state law). In South Carolina, 97 percent of obstetricians reported in 1997 that they "routinely screen women for HIV" (Bell, 1997). Whether this screening includes an actual HIV antibody test or is just the providers' judgment about the women's likely risk is unclear.

In 1997, 94 percent of New Jersey providers reported offering HIV testing to all or most patients (Ching, Paul, and Goldman, 1997). Anecdotal reports from the state, however, suggest that providers are more likely to offer HIV tests to women of color in urban areas that have been hardest hit with HIV/AIDS and far less likely to do so for white, suburban women. In fact, anecdotal reports from across the nation suggest that physician reluctance to offer testing is a major stumbling block to perinatal transmission efforts. The IOM committee heard several explanations of why physicians may not be offering HIV counseling and testing. First, physicians feel that if they are to give women an HIV test, they must do so only with appropriate pre- and posttest counseling; some say that the current CDC (1995) recommendations take at least fifteen to twenty minutes per person. Since for many practices the yield of this testing is low and demands for time are high, it is difficult to justify the time for testing along with the standard counseling and testing procedure. Second, many prenatal care providers serving low-HIV-prevalence populations are concerned that they do not have the expertise to treat women who test positive or even to interpret the test results or refer the woman for appropriate care. Finally, providers express concern that raising the issue of an HIV test would be embarrassing (to themselves and the women they serve) because the discussion necessarily involves sexual behavior and drug use and may be interpreted as the provider's suggesting that the woman has some of the risk factors for HIV infection.

The result of the practices discussed above is that 60 to 94 percent of women in eleven states studied in CDC's Perinatal Guidelines Evaluation Project (PGEP) were offered an HIV test during the course of their prenatal care (Centers for Disease Control, 1998). The proportion of perinatally HIV-exposed children who received or whose mothers received any AZT increased rapidly through 1995 but reached a plateau at 80 to 85 percent.

Acceptance of AZT Treatment. There are very few evaluation data on the acceptance of AZT by pregnant women. In the PGEP study, 75 to 86 percent of women accepted AZT when offered (Institute of Medicine, 1999). Anecdotal evidence suggests that the acceptance rate is almost 100 percent if the treatment is strongly endorsed by the women's physician with appropriate counseling. In the four-state CDC study, only 5 percent of women refused AZT when offered and only 6 percent discontinued AZT during pregnancy once started (Centers for Disease Control, 1998).

In summary, it seems that there are two weak links in the chain of causality that provide opportunities for enhanced prevention programs: increased use of prenatal care and efforts to ensure that prenatal care providers offer HIV testing to their patients. Increasing access to prenatal care has been a national priority for decades, so it was not clear that additional efforts would be effective in reaching the relatively few women, mostly urban minorities and many who use drugs, not yet receiving prenatal care. To address this group, the IOM committee suggested that rapid HIV tests, which could be used during labor and delivery with time to start treatment if a woman tests positive, be considered. Offering HIV tests to more women already in prenatal care, on the other hand, seemed more feasible, especially given the explanation of why providers do not offer it now. The committee therefore broadened its evaluation to include the economic and ethical aspects of a population-based HIV screening program in prenatal care.

Economic Evaluation of Prenatal HIV Screening and Treatment. There have been a number of economic evaluations of HIV testing and treatment in pregnancy, each with different assumptions and different specific questions (Gorsky and others, 1996; Mauskopf and others, 1996; Myers, Thompson, and Simpson, 1998; and others since the publication of the IOM report). Taken as a group, however, they generally establish the cost-effectiveness of prenatal HIV screening and treatment programs.

Mauskopf and others (1996), for instance, have estimated the economic impact of treating pregnant women who are HIV positive with AZT and found that such treatment is cost-saving over a wide range of assumptions. They furthermore found that voluntary prenatal HIV screening programs are generally cost-saving if the prevalence of HIV in pregnant women exceeds 4.6 per 1,000. Under the assumption that the prevalence rate is 1.7 per 1,000 (the national average), the cost per case prevented of a voluntary screening program with comprehensive counseling and 100 percent acceptance is $155,000. The same program with limited pretest counseling is actually cost-saving (Mauskopf and others, 1996).

The IOM committee, however, was interested in the cost-effectiveness of universal, routine HIV testing in prenatal care (Institute of Medicine, 1999). Two assumptions are needed for this calculation. First, the marginal cost of including an HIV test in the standard prenatal test panel was estimated to be $3.00 to $5.00 per woman. Costs of testing vary markedly according to the circumstances in which the testing is done. ELISA tests (the standard first-line HIV test) done by private laboratories range from $15.00 to $65.00, but the cost to state laboratories of doing an HIV test on a specimen already in hand is less than $5.00. It costs the U.S. Army only $2.50 per serum specimen in its routine screening of all recruits because of the number tested and the established infrastructure for transporting the specimens to the laboratory (Mauskopf and others, 1996). In New York State, the marginal cost of testing infant heel-stick samples for HIV is only about $1.00 (G. S. Birkhead, personal communication, 1998). Second, the follow-up cost for a repeatedly positive ELISA test (including the cost of the Western blot confirmatory test and counseling those who are positive, but not treatment costs) is $100.00.

Standard HIV testing uses a two-stage procedure (Pins, Teruya, and Stowell, 1997). A specimen is subjected to an initial ELISA test; it if is positive, it is subjected to a second. If it is repeatedly positive, the same specimen is subjected to a confirmatory Western blot test. The sensitivity of the repeated ELISA test is 100 percent, and the specificity is 0.999 (Pins, Teruya, and Stowell, 1997). The IOM assumed that the prevalence of HIV in pregnant women ranges from 1 per 10,000 to 500 per 10,000. This range parallels the range of values in the 1994 Survey of Childbearing Women (Davis and others, 1995).

The IOM analysis displayed the number of true positives (women truly HIV positive) and the number of positive ELISA tests that would result for every 10,000 pregnant women tested for a given prevalence rate. It also showed the positive predictive value (PPV) of the test—that is, the probability that a person who tests positive does in fact have the condition. As is generally the case, the PPV is lower where the prevalence of HIV is also low and increases as the prevalence increases. If the prevalence of HIV in the population tested is above 20 per 10,000 (as is the case in about seven states, the District of Columbia, and Puerto Rico), the PPV exceeds 67 percent. If the prevalence is as low as 2 per 10,000 (as is the case in Utah and Oklahoma), the PPV is only about 17 percent. This means that there is less than a one in five chance that a woman with a repeatedly positive ELISA test is truly infected with HIV. These rates apply to repeated ELISA testing only. When the original blood samples are subjected to Western blot confirmatory testing, most of the false-positive results would become negative. Some fraction of Western blot results is indeterminate (depending on the testing procedure used and the laboratory), but some of these indicate an early-stage infection (Pins, Teruya, and Stowell, 1997).

The IOM also evaluated the marginal cost of prenatal testing (per 10,000 women in prenatal care) and the cost per true positive case found. The results show that in high-prevalence areas, the cost per case found is extremely low—hundreds of dollars. Even in low-prevalence areas, the cost exceeds $50,000 per case found only if the marginal cost per ELISA test is $5 and the prevalence is 1 per 10,000. In a more reasonable, low-prevalence scenario ($3 per test and a prevalence of 2 per 10,000), the cost per case found is only $15,600. These numbers are not precise, but they nevertheless clearly indicate that universal routine HIV testing integrated into prenatal care can be very cost-effective, even in low-prevalence areas.

Ethical Analysis of Public Health Screening Programs

Disease screening is one of the most basic tools of modern public health and preventive medicine. As screening programs have been implemented over the years, a substantial body of experience has been gained. To capitalize from this experience, the IOM committee reviewed the experience in the United States with perinatal screening for syphilis, phenylketonuria, sickle cell disease, neural tube defects, and prenatal and newborn screening for substance abuse. Based on this review, the committee concluded that when screening is conducted in contexts of gender inequality, racial discrimination, sexual taboos, and poverty, these conditions shape the attitudes and beliefs of the health system and public health decision makers as well as patients, including those who have lost confidence that the health care system will treat them fairly. Thus, if screening programs are poorly conceived, organized, or implemented, they may lead to interventions of questionable merit and the vulnerability of groups and individuals. Through the experience with public health screening programs, a series of characteristics of well-organized public health screening programs has evolved (Wilson and Jungner, 1968).

The IOM committee's summary of the relevant characteristics is as follows:

1. The goals of the screening program should be clearly specified and shown to be achievable.
2. The natural history of the condition should be adequately understood, and treatment or intervention for those found positive widely accepted

by the scientific and medical community, with evidence that early inter-vention improves health outcomes.
3. The screening test or measurement should distinguish those individuals who are likely to have the condition from those who are unlikely to have it.
4. There should be adequate facilities for diagnosis and resources for treat-ment for all who are found to have the condition, as well as agreement as to who will treat them.
5. The test and possible interventions should be acceptable to the affected population.

Recommendations

To meet the goal that all pregnant women be tested for HIV as early in preg-nancy as possible, and those who are positive remain in care so that they can receive optimal treatment for themselves and their children, the IOM committee's central recommendation was a national policy of universal HIV testing, with patient notification, as a routine component of prenatal care.

There are two key elements to the committee's recommendation. The first is that HIV screening should be routine with notification. This means that the test for HIV would be integrated into the standard battery of pre-natal tests and women would be informed that the HIV test is being conducted and of their right to refuse it. This element addresses the doctor-patient relationship and can reduce barriers to patient acceptance of HIV testing. Most important, this approach preserves the right of the woman to refuse the test. If it is followed, women would not have to deal with the burden of disclosing personal risks or potential stereotyping; the test would simply be a part of prenatal care that is the same for everyone. Routine testing will also reduce burdens on providers such as the need for costly extensive pretest counseling and having discussions about personal risks that many providers think are embarrassing. A policy of routine test-ing might also help to reduce physicians' risk of liability to women and children, where providers incorrectly guess that a woman is not at risk for HIV infection.

The second key element to the recommendation is that screening should be universal, meaning that it applies to all pregnant women, regardless of their risk factors and the prevalence rates where they live. The benefit of uni-versal screening is that it ameliorates the stigma associated with being sin-gled out for testing, and it overcomes the problem that many HIV-infected women are missed when a risk-based or prevalence-based testing strategy is employed (Barbacci, Repke, and Chaisson, 1991).

Making prenatal HIV testing universal also has broad social implica-tions. First, if it is incorporated into standard prenatal testing procedures, the costs of screening are low and the benefits are high. Assuming that the marginal cost of adding an ELISA test to the current prenatal panel is $3 per woman and the prevalence of HIV in pregnant women is 2 per 10,000, the cost of routine prenatal testing is $15,600 per HIV-positive woman found. Even if the cost of the test is $5 and the prevalence 1 per 10,000, the cost per case found is $51,100. Taken in the context of the cost of caring for an HIV-infected child, although not all women found to be HIV positive will benefit, these figures indicate the clear benefits of routine prenatal HIV testing.

Second, universal screening is the only way to deal with possible geographic shifts in the epidemiology of perinatal transmission. Although perinatal AIDS cases are currently concentrated in eastern states, particularly New York, New Jersey, and Florida, there have been shifts in the prevalence of HIV in pregnant women, including an increase in the South in the early 1990s. Changes in the regional demographics of drug use can also lead to changes in the distribution of HIV infection in pregnant women. Given the uncertainty of these trends, the committee considered universal testing the most prudent method to reduce perinatal transmission despite possible regional fluctuations.

Third, it would help to reduce stigmatization of groups by calling attention to a communicable disease that does not have inherent geographic barriers or a genetic predisposition. Focusing on the communicable disease aspect may allow national education programs that would otherwise be difficult, discouraging infected individuals from hiding themselves and thus not benefiting from care, and discouraging a "blame the victim" mentality.

Recently the American College of Obstetricians and Gynecologists and the American Academy of Pediatrics (1999) issued a joint statement that essentially adopts the approach in the IOM report. The next year, the CDC (2000) issued draft guidelines for HIV testing and treatment in prenatal care that also adopt the basic recommendation of the IOM report.

The Value of the Evaluation

The IOM's report was an evaluation in two senses of the word. First, reflecting its congressional charge, the committee evaluated the efforts to prevent perinatal transmission of HIV through the implementation of plans based on the ACTG 076 findings. This phase of the evaluation was focused on process and outcomes and relied in large part on ad hoc studies carried out by epidemiologists and health service researchers in public health departments and academic institutions. Since most were not published in the scientific literature, their validity is sometimes hard to determine, and taken individually, many were not very convincing. Nevertheless, in conjunction with a series of workshops, site visits, and interviews that it organized, the IOM committee felt that a consistent picture emerged. The central conclusion of this analysis was that the failure of providers to offer HIV testing in prenatal care was an important and easily addressable part of the problem.

The IOM report was also an evaluation of a proposed policy, universal HIV testing, with notification, as a routine component of prenatal care. Having established that offering HIV testing was the problem, the evaluation focused on the economic and ethical aspects of this proposed policy. Because the proposed policy was not yet in place, much of the evaluation had to be based on theoretical concerns and experience extrapolated from other perinatal prevention programs.

The results of the IOM evaluation were surprising because the idea of targeting is firmly ingrained in public health and preventive medicine education and practice. The purpose of identifying risk factors, we are taught in epidemiology, is twofold: to modify those that are changeable and to target programs to populations with unmodifiable risk factors. Moreover, because prevention programs essentially involve treating many people who are not destined to get the problem that the program aims to prevent, program costs can easily exceed benefits if programs are targeted at the wrong groups.

Prenatal HIV screening illustrates the problems with this single-minded perspective by clarifying the downsides of targeting programs: stigma, discrimination, and disenfranchisement. No one wants to be the target of a weapon, and public health programs that are not properly conceived and implemented can have this effect. In the case of perinatal transmission of HIV, the overall low cost of a screening program even in low-prevalence areas, combined with the high costs of targeting vulnerable women, outweighs the epidemiologist's instinct to target the populations most at risk.

There is a sense, however, in which the IOM analysis supports a kind of targeting because the focus is on programs, not people. A simple analysis in the IOM report compares the effect of increasing use of prenatal care with increased offering of the HIV test by prenatal care providers. Consider a hypothetical population of 7,000 HIV-infected childbearing women (approximately the number giving birth in the United States in a year). Current estimates are that 85 percent of HIV-infected women obtain prenatal care, 75 percent are counseled and offered an HIV test, and 80 percent of those who are offered accept the test. Coupled with additional assumptions about the percentage of women who are offered and accept treatment and the transmission rate in women with and without treatment, it is estimated that a goal of 350 infected children is achievable, compared with an estimated 1,072 with no further intervention. With these assumptions, increasing the proportion of women who receive prenatal care to 100 percent results in 9 fewer children born with HIV infection. Increasing providers' offering of the HIV test alone, on the other hand, results in 16 fewer infected children, and increasing the proportion of women who accept the test by itself results in 12 fewer infected children. Since major changes in HIV test offering and acceptance seem possible with a relatively minor, low-cost policy change (universal routine HIV testing, with notification), this policy compares favorably with efforts to increase the use of prenatal care, which are likely to be costly and ineffective, given that policymakers for more than two decades have tried to address this problem and women who currently get no prenatal care are likely to be a difficult group to serve.

References

American Academy of Pediatrics and American College of Obstetricians and Gynecologists. "Joint Statement of the American Academy of Pediatrics and the American College of Obstetricians and Gynecologists." *Pediatrics*, 1999, *104*, 128.

Barbacci, M., Repke, J. T., and Chaisson, R. E. "Routine Prenatal Screening for HIV Infection." *Lancet*, 1991, *337*, 709–711.

Bell, L. J. "Survey of Prenatal Care Providers' Screening Practices." *EPINotes: Disease Prevention and Epidemiology Newsletter*, 1997, *19*, 1–2.

Centers for Disease Control and Prevention. "U.S. Public Health Service Recommendations for Human Immunodeficiency Virus Counseling and Voluntary Testing for Pregnant Women." *Morbidity and Mortality Weekly Report*, 1995, *44*(RR-7).

Centers for Disease Control and Prevention. "The Changing Demographics of HIV." *HIV/AIDS Surveillance Report*, 1996, *8*(2).

Centers for Disease Control and Prevention. "Challenges for Targeting HIV Prevention Programs." *HIV/AIDS Surveillance Report*, *9*(2), 1997a.

Centers for Disease Control and Prevention. "Update: Perinatally Acquired HIV/AIDS—United States, 1997." *Morbidity and Mortality Weekly Report*, 1997b, *46*, 1086–1092.

Centers for Disease Control and Prevention. "Success in Implementing PHS Guidelines to Reduce Perinatal Transmission of HIV—Louisiana, Michigan, New Jersey, South Carolina, 1993, 1995, and 1996." *Morbidity and Mortality Weekly Report*, 1998, *47*(33), 688–691.

Centers for Disease Control and Prevention. *Revised U.S. Public Health Services Recommendations from Human Immunodeficiency Virus Screening of Pregnant Women. Draft Revised Guidelines*. Atlanta, Ga.: Centers for Disease Control and Prevention, 2000.

Ching, S., Paul, S., and Goldman, K. *The Diffusion of HIV Counseling Among New Jersey Obstetricians and Gynecologists: Factors Influencing Levels of Implementation*. New Brunswick: New Jersey Graduate Program in Public Health, Fieldwork Project, May 1997.

Connor, E. M., and others. "Reduction of Maternal-Infant Transmission of Human Immunodeficiency Virus Type 1 with Zidovudine Treatment. Pediatric AIDS Clinical Trials Group Protocol 076 Study Group." *New England Journal of Medicine*, 1994, *331*, 1173–1180.

Davis, S. F., and others. "Prevalence and Incidence of Vertically Acquired HIV Infection in the United States." *Journal of American Medical Association*, 1995, *274*(12), 952–955.

Gorsky, R. D., and others. "Preventing Perinatal Transmission of HIV: Costs and Effectiveness of a Recommended Intervention." *Public Health Reports*, 1996, *111*(4), 335–341.

Institute of Medicine. Committee on Perinatal Transmission of HIV. *Reducing the Odds: Preventing Perinatal Transmission of HIV in the United States*. Washington, D.C.: National Academy Press, 1999.

International Perinatal HIV Group. "The Mode of Delivery and the Risk of Vertical Transmission of Human Immunodeficiency Virus Type 1—A Meta-Analysis of 15 Prospective Cohort Studies." *New England Journal of Medicine*, 1999, *340*, 977–987.

Mauskopf, J. A., and others. "Economic Impact of Treatment of HIV-Positive Pregnant Women and Their Newborns with Zidovudine: Implications for HIV Screening." *Journal of the American Medical Association*, 1996, *276*(2), 132–138.

Michigan Department of Community Health. *Improving the Odds: Reducing Perinatal HIV Transmission: Report of the Recommendations of the Maternal Child Health Advisory Committee, Subcommittee on Perinatal HIV Reduction*. Lansing: Michigan Department of Community Health, 1997.

Montana Department of Public Health and Human Services. Communicable Disease Control and Prevention Bureau, STD/HIV Section. *DPHHS HIV Screening Survey Results*. Helena: Montana Department of Public Health and Human Services, 1996.

Myers, E. R., Thompson, J. W., and Simpson, K. "Cost-Effectiveness of Mandatory Compared with Voluntary Screening for Human Immunodeficiency Virus in Pregnancy." *Obstetrics and Gynecology*, 1998, *91*(2), 164–181.

National Center for Health Statistics. *Health: United States, 1996–1997, and Injury Chartbook*. Hyattsville, Md.: National Center for Health Statistics, 1997.

Newton, Z. B., and Bell, W. C. "HIV Perinatal Prevention Project: Contact and Survey of Metro Atlanta Obstetricians." Paper presented to the Georgia Obstetrical and Gynecological Society, July 21, 1997.

Pins, M. R., Teruya, J., and Stowell, C. P. "Human Immunodeficiency Virus Testing and Case Detection: Pragmatic and Technical Issues." In D. Cotton and D. H. Watts (eds.), *The Medical Management of AIDS in Women*. New York: Wiley-Liss, 1996.

Riley, C. W. *Perinatal HIV Infection White Paper*. Richmond: Virginia Department of Health, Division of STD/AIDS, Jan. 1998.

Rosenberg, K. D., and others. "HIV Screening Practices of Oregon Prenatal Care Providers." Abstract. Eugene: Center for Disease Prevention and Epidemiology, Oregon Health Division, n.d.

Segal, A. I. "Physician Attitudes Toward Human Immunodeficiency Virus Testing in Pregnancy." *American Journal of Obstetrics and Gynecology*, 1996, *174*(6), 1750–1756.

U.S. Department of Health and Human Services. *Natality: Vital Statistics of the United States* (Vol. 1). Hyattsville Md.: National Center for Health Statistics, 1992.

Ventura, S. J., Martin, J. A., Curtin, S. C., and Mathews, T. J. "Report of Final Natality Statistics, 1996." *Monthly Vital Statistics*, 1998, *4*(11), 43.

Wilson, J.M.G., and Jungner, F. *Principles and Practice of Screening for Disease*. Geneva: World Health Organization, 1968.

Wortley, P. M., and Fleming, P. L. "AIDS in Women in the United States." *Journal of the American Medical Association*, 1997, *278*(11), 911–916.

MICHAEL A. STOTO *is professor and chair of the Department of Epidemiology and Biostatistics, George Washington University Medical Center.*

5

Cost-effectiveness analyses, especially in education, are too rare. Yet they offer powerful and valuable insights for evaluators and can provide information that is counter to common sense, popular appeal, and traditional ideas.

Waiting for Godot: Cost-Effectiveness Analysis in Education

Henry M. Levin

For more than thirty years I have been applying cost-effectiveness and cost-benefit analysis to education. When I began this work in about 1970, there were almost no cost-effectiveness studies reported in the literature, and the term was not found in education at all. The term *cost-effectiveness* is now commonly used in justifying specific educational interventions. It has also become standard parlance among educational policymakers and decision makers.

Ostensible concerns for cost-effectiveness in education are not surprising. The educational sector of the United States is second in size only to the health care sector in terms of its drain on national resources. It is considerably larger than the military sector. When one includes formal education and the various forms of training, it has been estimated that about 10 percent of the gross domestic product—about three-quarters of a trillion dollars in 1998—is allocated to education, encompassing formal education and various forms of training (Merrill-Lynch, 1999). These are massive sums, and they do not include the considerable opportunity costs of lost output for society resulting from student participation in education and training rather than the workplace.

At the same time, there have been persistent concerns about the efficiency of educational spending. Hanushek (1986, 1997) has used results from educational production functions to argue that elementary and secondary schools allocate their resources in a highly inefficient way. Although his interpretations have been challenged by Krueger (2000), no one has argued that educational spending is highly efficient. Indeed, at least one of the reasons for the movement toward charter schools and vouchers is the

NEW DIRECTIONS FOR EVALUATION, no. 90, Summer 2001   © Jossey-Bass, A Publishing Unit of John Wiley & Sons, Inc.   55 view that changes in the organization of education and the use of market incentives will improve the effectiveness of resource use in education. And there is considerable criticism of the effectiveness of elementary and secondary schools, particular for minorities, immigrants, and the poor. In higher education, there are serious challenges with regard to both costs and productivity. Tuition costs and state subsidies per student have risen at a faster rate than inflation, and there are no obvious improvements in productivity (Groccia and Miller 1998).

At the same time, evaluators and public policy analysts have an important tool to guide resource allocation: cost-effectiveness analysis. Cost-effectiveness analysis provides a method of comparing alternatives for their relative costs and results and providing guidelines on which of the alternatives provides the most impact relative to cost. It differs from its close relation, cost-benefit analysis, which requires monetary measures of impact relative to costs. Most endeavors to improve education are unable to use cost-benefit analysis because it is difficult to measure the values of the improvements in market terms or benefits. But it is possible to measure academic achievement and other measures of school quality and effectiveness. Accordingly, cost-effectiveness analysis enables measures of learning, as well as other appropriate indicators to be used to assess educational outcomes relative to costs.

Cost-effectiveness analysis emerged in the 1960s as an important method for choosing among costly weapons systems. Gradually the tools of cost-effectiveness analysis made their way from the Pentagon to other government agencies with President Lyndon Johnson's requirement that all budgetary requests be supported by a program-planning-budgeting system that tied mission and goals to costs. Over subsequent decades, advances were made in refining the techniques and improving their user-friendliness (Levin, 1975). A particularly strong expansion of cost-effectiveness analysis is found in the evaluation of health services (Drummond, O'Brien, Stoddart, and Torrance, 1997; Gold, Siegel, Russell, and Weinstein, 1996). In the health domain, some efforts have been particularly ambitious. For example, the State of Oregon attempted to use the tool to ascertain the priority and reimbursement rates of state-supported medical procedures (Eddy, 1991). The World Bank undertook a massive and comprehensive study to guide resource allocation for twenty-four categories of health interventions for disease control in developing countries by using a cost-effectiveness framework (Jamison, Mosley, Measham, and Bobadilla, 1993).

And apparently cost-effectiveness evaluators have been busy in education. A November 2000 search of the Education Resources Information Center (ERIC), a database funded by the federal government, located about 11,800 articles, reports, and other documents addressing cost-effectiveness in education. This was about 2,400 items greater than a similar search revealed in 1996, suggesting an increase of 600 each year. Thus, it would appear that cost-effectiveness studies in education are both much in demand

and much in supply through the efforts of evaluators. But on closer inspection, there is much less than meets the eye. Surprisingly, there seems to be neither an abundant database of literature on cost-effectiveness in education nor much of a demand for such studies.

This chapter shows that what seems to be a surprise should not be surprising to policymakers. It focuses on the dearth of cost-effectiveness studies in education, despite the large numbers of studies that use cost-effectiveness jargon, and the reasons that the tool has not flourished as it has in the area of health care, as well as some ways of promoting its use.

What Is Cost-Effectiveness Analysis in Evaluation?

Cost-effectiveness analysis refers to a method for combining appropriate measures of outcomes with costs so that program and policy alternatives can be ranked according to their effectiveness relative to resource use. Presumably the alternatives with the least cost relative to their results (or best results relative to costs) are the ones that are most attractive for adoption. This information should be viewed as helpful in guiding, but not determining, decisions. Other issues such as implementation feasibility need to be considered in the decision process (Levin and McEwan, 2000).

Most of the public policy audience and professional evaluators would agree that cost-effectiveness should be taken into account in decision making. But while this audience is usually very circumspect when it comes to estimating the effectiveness of alternatives, it is completely lax when referring to costs. The path that is often followed is based on the assumption that budgets or expenditure statements contain the requisite information and that it is necessary only to read the appropriate figures from such statements or get an accountant or manager to provide the right numbers. Unfortunately, estimation of costs requires a set of methodological procedures that must be followed to obtain accurate and consistent cost estimates, just as studies of effectiveness require such procedures. In general, there are three steps to designing and implementing a cost analysis. (For details, see Levin and McEwan, 2000.)

First, the resources or ingredients are identified that are required for each alternative. These details are fundamental, before any monetary values are attempted. Basically they respond to the question of what resources were required that accounted for the levels of effectiveness of each of the alternatives. The precise types of personnel are specified according to their qualifications and time commitments. A similar exercise is carried out for facilities, equipment, and other program inputs, as well as for client resources. Details on ingredients are obtained from descriptive reports, observations, and interviews.

Once the ingredients are set out, it is possible to place values on them. To as great an extent as possible, market prices for each ingredient are derived for each and used to value them. In many cases, the ingredient will not be obtained through a market transaction such as space in a building that is owned by the sponsoring entity or in-kind resources such as volunteer time. In those cases, so-called shadow prices—the estimated value of the resource based on an alternative procedure—are used. Although some of these costs can be obtained from expenditure information, much of that information will be incomplete or inappropriate, so one must be exceedingly cautious in ascertaining precisely how expenditures are accounted for by these sources.

Once the costs of individual ingredients are obtained, they can be summed to estimate the total cost of each alternative. In education, these are normally viewed on a per-student or per-participant basis (average cost) to compare effectiveness per unit of cost among alternatives. At the same time, it is important to analyze the distribution of the burden of costs among different sponsoring entities as well as clients to find out who pays the costs for each alternative. Cost information is combined with effectiveness to make cost-effectiveness comparisons. Similarly, the same type of cost analysis can be used to compare alternatives on a cost-benefit or cost-utility basis if appropriate data on benefits or utilities are available. The main point here is that cost analysis must be treated methodically just as effectiveness analysis is. It is not a casual activity or a rhetorical one.

Cost-Effectiveness Studies in Education

About thirty years ago, I started my own sojourn in this field. I wanted to establish cost-effectiveness analysis as a useful evaluative and policy tool in the field of education and the other areas of human service. As an early demonstration, I used data from the Coleman Report (1966) to compare the cost-effectiveness of two alternative strategies for teacher selection: hiring more experienced teachers or those with higher verbal test scores. The results suggested that it was from five to ten times as effective per unit of cost to raise student achievement by getting more verbally able teachers than those with greater experience. I followed this with a cost-benefit study for getting all students to high school completion. This study suggested that the benefits of such an accomplishment were seven times as high as the costs and that the returns in higher government revenues exceeded government costs by a ratio of two to one.

Three decades ago, it was obvious that the use of cost-effectiveness analysis to judge educational interventions was not of much interest to economists. The field of economics of education was derived from human capital theory and was devoted primarily to the estimation of rates of return to educational investments rather than efficiency in institutional resource allocation by level of education. Of course, rate-of-return analysis is a form of cost-benefit analysis, but not one that is very useful for reviewing the effectiveness of educational interventions designed to improve student achievement. Even today, rate-of-return analysis is far more prominent than cost-effectiveness research in the field of education. Educational evaluators were preoccupied with educational effectiveness, regardless of cost implications. It seemed that a major priority should be the integration of costs with effectiveness measures to rank alternatives according to their efficiency in resource use. Because economists showed little interest, I saw the appropriate response as convincing educational evaluators to add cost analyses to their evaluation tool kits. My hope was that cost-effectiveness studies would make their way into the emerging field of social evaluation.

What was needed was a systematic method of measuring costs that could be integrated with effectiveness research to establish cost-effectiveness comparisons. Early in the 1970s, I worked to develop a method to undertake cost-effectiveness analyses by evaluators. This method took the form of estimating costs on a financial spreadsheet, incorporating the three steps set out above. The work was published for an evaluator audience in the first *Handbook of Evaluation Research* (Levin, 1975). Evaluators expressed great interest in learning more, so I devoted myself to a book-length treatment of the subject (Levin, 1983). This book had strong sales (ultimately thirteen printings), suggesting wide interest in the field.

Despite the substantial sales of the book, the actual presence of cost-effectiveness evaluations in education was minimal. A survey that I did for the years 1985 through 1988 found that less than 1 percent of the presentations at the annual meetings of the American Evaluation Association used cost-effectiveness analysis or included it as a component of evaluations, and the topic was virtually invisible at the annual meetings of the American Educational Research Association during those years (Levin, 1991). Monk and King (1993) chose two scholarly journals to compare for their coverage of cost-effectiveness analysis over a five-year period in the late 1980s and early 1990s. *Educational Evaluation and Policy Analysis* (EEPA), a journal of the American Educational Research Association, is the main general outlet for studies of educational evaluation. The *Journal of Policy Analysis and Management* (JPAM), sponsored by the Association for Public Policy Analysis and Management, is a broader journal covering many policy fields. Both journals are highly refereed, so one would expect what was published to be of high quality. Although 80 percent of the JPAM articles dealt with explicit issues of cost, only 25 percent of the EEPA articles were in that category. This does not mean that the articles provided fully developed cost-effectiveness studies, only that they addressed costs.

In 1996 the preparation of the second edition of the cost-effectiveness book provided me and my coauthor, Patrick McEwan, with the opportunity to revisit the literature to see what had been accomplished since publication of the first edition in 1983. McEwan surveyed a wide base of literature for potential case studies and examples of cost-effectiveness analysis in education. In checking all of the standard literature sources in economics, education, and public policy, he found very few cost-effectiveness studies in education generally and no great upsurge for recent years. In contrast, the health literature was replete with a very large number of cost-effectiveness studies and a wide acceptance of the tool in the evaluation literature in that field (summaries are found in Drummond, O'Brien, Stoddart, and Torrance, 1997; Gold, Siegel, Russell, and Weinstein,1996; Sloan, 1995).

At the same time, William Clune of the University of Wisconsin undertook a study of the methodological strengths and policy usefulness of published research on cost-effectiveness in education (Clune, 1999). (I was an adviser on the study.) Using the ERIC database for studies incorporating the term *cost-effectiveness,* Clune found over 9,000 titles. The sheer volume of studies using that key word was in sharp contrast to the few studies that we had uncovered. Limiting the search to 1991 through 1996, he found 1,329 titles. Abstracts of the studies were obtained and allocated among four categories according to apparent methodological rigor:

Rhetorical—cost-effectiveness claims with no data on either costs or effects
Minimal—minimal data, such as potential categories of effectiveness or cost
   feasibility with no evidence of systematic study
Substantial attempt—attempt to mount data on cost and effectiveness but
   with serious flaws, such as effectiveness design or cost measurement
Plausible—ingredients or resource approach to costs and a strong effectiveness design with comparisons among alternatives

In order to make the survey manageable, Clune removed studies that did not focus on outcomes of elementary and secondary education. This reduced the sample to 541 studies. Based on the abstracts, he found that more than 80 percent of the studies were rhetorical (56 percent) or minimal (27 percent). Only 1 percent were plausible, and another 1 percent were between substantial and plausible, with the remaining 15 percent being substantial. Clune asked me to provide an independent rating of studies in his sample. We found that his ratings were more generous than mine.

Clune then proceeded to an evaluation of a 10 percent sample of the full studies to confirm whether ratings from the abstracts were consistent with ratings of the full studies. The initial distribution of ratings of the abstracts was similar to the pattern of ratings of the full studies, with only minor changes. He found that none of the full studies reached the top category, and slightly fewer would be placed in the bottom two categories (70 percent rather than 80 percent). The average rating based on readings of the full studies was 1.93, indicating something better than rhetorical but not quite minimal. Most important was the fact that there was very little cost-effectiveness analysis in the body of literature that claimed to have findings on cost-effectiveness in education. Overall, this does not suggest great confidence in studies that claim to have produced cost-effectiveness results.

Perhaps most discouraging is the fact that even when recognized scholars claim to do cost-effectiveness studies, they often shortchange the cost analysis. That is, the same persons who have great concern for the validity and implementation of evaluation designs of effectiveness and reliability of measures ignore completely the methodology of cost analysis in making cost-effectiveness claims. Two recent examples of interesting studies by well-known scholars are informative. Mayer and Peterson (1999), in their book on school reform, provide a summary chapter on costs and benefits of school reforms. But they measure both costs and benefits in a cursory manner, and they derive the putative benefits of the effectiveness from systematic studies.

Their estimate of the cost of class size reduction, for example, is not based on any cost study at all. Instead, the authors determine costs by such steps as "assuming annual compensation of $44,000" for teacher compensation and assuming that classrooms "might represent roughly a third the cost of additional personnel" (p. 351). No justification or data set is provided that supports these assumptions. Moreover, the reputations of these authors in evaluation work suggest that neither would be likely to choose the effectiveness of an intervention by virtue of assumption. Indeed, they have ignored the systematic methods that have been developed for estimating costs, and the cost-effectiveness studies exist that have compared reductions in class size with other interventions (Levin, Glass, and Meister, 1987). Costs of school choice programs are given as "none," although the cost analysis of a prototype voucher system has suggested considerable costs beyond the existing system for record keeping, transportation, information, and adjudication (Levin and Driver 1997).

This relative dearth of cost-analysis studies in education and the poor quality of what does exist represent a puzzle, especially in comparison with the quantity and strength of the cost-effectiveness literature in health.

Explaining the Paradox

It is not easy to explain this phenomenon. What may appear to be causes may also be consequences. For example, we may find that there is a lack of training among educational evaluators in the methods of cost-effectiveness analysis. But if there is not much demand for such studies among policymakers, it would not be surprising to find few studies and little training in an area that is of low priority. Nevertheless, there are possible explanations.

Lack of Training. Because evaluations in education are done primarily by persons who consider themselves to be evaluation specialists, it is useful to review both training programs and textbooks. To my knowledge, there is no system for ranking systematically the various programs of preparation for educational evaluation. Accordingly, I compiled a list of these programs by soliciting the opinions of three noted educational evaluators. This list is not complete, but it is probably representative of the better-known programs preparing evaluation specialists in education. The list includes programs (in alphabetical order) at Arizona State, the University of California at Berkeley, the University of Colorado, Columbia, Harvard, the University of Michigan,

Northwestern, Stanford, the University of California at Los Angeles, Vanderbilt, and the University of Wisconsin. I checked both the course catalogues and the Web sites for information on each of these programs to ascertain whether some training was required in cost-effectiveness analysis. Although each program listed some course requirements, I could not find a single program that required a course or training in cost-effectiveness. In fact, in my thirty-one years as a member of the faculty at Stanford University, I was unable to convince my colleagues that evaluation experts need training in cost-effectiveness analysis. In summary, cost-effectiveness analysis is viewed as unnecessary for training educational evaluation specialists.

I also reviewed the top master's programs in public health as listed by *U.S. News and World Report*. These included, in descending order of ratings, Johns Hopkins, Harvard, the University of North Carolina, the University of Michigan, the University of Washington, Columbia, the University of California at Berkeley, the University of California at Los Angeles, the University of Minnesota, and Yale. Virtually all of these schools have a program in health policy that requires a course in finance and one in health policy administration. Calls to three of these schools revealed that cost-effectiveness analysis is covered in the health policy concentration. Based on this information and publications in the health evaluation literature, it is clear that training programs in the areas of public health seem to incorporate literature, studies, and methods of cost-effectiveness analysis, whereas the technique is virtually absent from evaluation training in education.

Additional confirmation of this finding is reflected in a search of textbooks used in courses on educational evaluation. A sampling of courses and instructors in the institutions already noted yielded the following books: Berk and Rossi (1990), Fink (1995), Patton (1997), Popham (1988), Rossi, Freeman, and Lipsey (1999), and Sax (1989). This list is incomplete but representative of the field. Patton (1997) is virtually devoid of cost-effectiveness methodology. Popham (1989) includes a 19-page chapter that provides little information beyond an introduction. Sax (1989), in its 678 pages, does not mention cost-effectiveness analysis, nor does Fink (1995). Rossi, Freeman, and Lipsey (1999) provide a full chapter on "measuring efficiency." The chapter is an excellent introduction but does not provide training or skills in doing cost-effectiveness analysis. Berk and Rossi (1990) barely mention the subject. In most of these textbooks, the subject of cost-effectiveness analysis is nonexistent or worthy only of superficial mention.

The evidence is consistent that training programs in educational evaluation do not require preparation in cost-effectiveness analysis and that the tool is probably not familiar to those teaching or working in the field of educational evaluation. This conclusion is also confirmed by the cursory treatment or complete absence of cost-effectiveness analysis in evaluation textbooks used for courses in educational evaluation.

Lack of Effects. A second plausible reason for the absence of cost-effectiveness analysis in educational evaluation is that most educational research does not provide an unambiguous estimate of effects. Many, if not most, rigorous studies seem to find statistically insignificant results or differences in effect sizes that are so small that they lack practical significance. Even when results are found, such as in studies of class size reduction (Grissmer, 1999) or differences in student achievement between public and private schools, the effectiveness of these interventions is usually subject to controversy. Clearly, if there are few evaluation results on effectiveness that are accepted in education, any cost analysis will be viewed as gratuitous. My reading of the evaluation research literature is that there is less than meets the eye. That is, there is a huge stock of educational research, but much of it is of poor quality or idiosyncratic so that it cannot be generalized. Nevertheless, there are still substantial numbers of good studies that show at least some replications. Thus, it is not clear how important this reason is for the lack of cost-effectiveness evaluations in education.

Lack of Demand by Policymakers. A third reason that might explain the lack of development of cost-effectiveness studies in educational evaluation is that policymakers do not demand them. Consider that a systematic study of program evaluation units in all fifty state departments of education in the early 1980s found that not only did such units lack the capacities to do such analyses, but they were not called on to do them (Smith and Smith, 1985). Interestingly, few inquiries or policy decisions in education use information on cost-effectiveness analysis as a criterion. Even government units with responsibilities for budgetary analysis rarely use the tool. For example, the California legislature's Legislative Analyst's Office evaluates prospective legislation and constitutional initiatives for financial and other consequences. But the financial implications are reviewed separately from the potential effectiveness and not compared with other alternatives for using such resources.

In fact, there is very little funding for educational research and evaluation. The field of education has nothing comparable to the National Institutes of Health with its annual budget of about $16 billion in 2000. In contrast, the federal budget for educational research and dissemination was about $350 million, of which a large share was addressed to dissemination. Furthermore, much of what is called educational research is actually the collection of data for statistical reports such as those of the National Center for Educational Statistics. Pharmaceutical companies and medical suppliers, two very large industries, invest their own money in health care research because of the large potential payoffs to cost-effective products and services. There is no counterpart in education. Even the recent trend toward privatization of education in the United States and for-profit educational management organizations seems to generate far greater investments by the industry in marketing than in evaluation, and there is little evidence of important contributions to the research literature from this source. Without considerable resources for research and evaluation in education, it is not only the field of cost-effectiveness in education that is constrained but also educational evaluation itself.

At bottom is the possibility that not only do decision makers ignore cost-effectiveness analysis in their decisions to allocate resources; they may also actually find that it is a distraction that they wish to avoid. After all, cost-effectiveness analysis results may appear to hinder their discretion. By providing comparative indicators of both results and costs, the information will tend to inhibit expenditures on alternatives that are costly relative to their effectiveness. For example, one study found that peer tutoring was far more cost-effective in increasing student achievement in reading and mathematics in elementary and secondary schools than computer-assisted instruction, longer school days, and longer school years (Levin, Glass, and Meister, 1987). In fact, longer school years seemed to be the least cost-effective of the alternatives, but California and other states have spent billions of dollars to increase the length of the school year by a few days a year. Computers were considered to be the new elixir for education, and smaller class sizes were popular among teachers, parents, and politicians. Ostensibly, there were no additional resources invested in peer tutoring, but the states and federal government enthusiastically reduced class size, increased the length of the school day, and promoted computers.

In this respect, cost-effectiveness results may even serve as a threat to decision makers by providing information that is counter to common sense, popular appeal, and support of particular constituencies. It also may promote solutions that can be adopted only at the local level, such as peer tutoring, in contrast to changing mechanically the formulas for class size and school sessions, which can be determined by legislative and congressional fiat.

Conclusion

Of the three hypotheses that might account for the lack of significant development of cost-effectiveness evaluation in education, two address the supply side of evaluation. The first is the lack of apparent capacity and training in the field. There is obviously some truth to this explanation. Few evaluators have the training to do a competent cost-effectiveness evaluation, training programs in and textbooks on evaluation are weak on cost-effectiveness, and economists have not selected cost-effectiveness as an important area in which they address school effectiveness. The other supply explanation is the lack of effectiveness results that can be relied on. Without good estimates of the effectiveness of alternatives, cost estimates would seem superfluous. There is some truth to each of these, but I argue that the main culprit is a lack of demand.

If there is not much demand for cost-effectiveness analysis or if it is even viewed as onerous by decision makers, this will influence considerably the opportunities and the priorities in training. More and better training is a necessary condition but not a sufficient one to develop the activity. The same is true for the explanation that educational research is often unable to identify effective alternatives. Clearly, better training of researchers and more investment in effectiveness research could address these issues. But effectiveness results for computer-assisted instruction, peer tutoring, longer school days, and class size reduction have shown a pattern of effectiveness that is fairly consistent (Levin, Glass, and Meister, 1987). Yet a cost-effectiveness study of these alternatives is in conflict with the policy directions that subsequently were chosen.

More spending on educational research is also a derivative finding. Why spend more on information that is unlikely to be used for policy? Indeed, this seems to be the key issue. If cost-effectiveness analysis has a contribution to make in a sector that is spending at least $2 billion a day and billions of dollars in student time, how can we get the tool to be used in policy and decision making? We must convince both agencies that support research and evaluation and decision makers who might be persuaded to use it to push for cost-effective analyses when they fund research and evaluation. In order to convince them, we must continue to demonstrate the value of cost-effectiveness analysis and show the potential cost savings of using more cost-effective approaches over ones that are less cost-effective. At the same time, we must educate policymakers and evaluation funders about what cost-effectiveness attempts to do. These entities need to have an intuitive—if not a formal—understanding of what an acceptable study requires. In addition, they need to reject the rhetorical assertions that particular alternatives or educational interventions are "cost-effective" when there is no study or only a very primitive one.

One possibility is that the further that policymakers are removed from educational decision making, the more they will rely on cost-effectiveness or cost-benefit studies. When they are close to the locus of decision making—for example, at the local level—they are heavily influenced by their own perceptions of effectiveness and cost-effectiveness of interventions. In addition, they are likely to be besieged by considerable pressures from local educational and political constituencies, often in the form of personal appeals by colleagues or parents. Thus, reliance on formal evaluations and analysis would seem to be superfluous. But when the decision making is remote from the experience of decision makers and is less directly influenced by constituents who will be affected directly by decisions, formal analysis is more attractive. Indeed, such analyses can be used to defuse the competing claims of lobbying groups.

Since more than 90 percent of educational spending is derived from state and local sources, this could provide a partial explanation of why there is so little demand for cost-effectiveness studies in elementary and secondary education. Where the federal government allocates all or most of the resources for a program, we would expect to see more sponsorship of cost-effectiveness or cost-benefit studies and their use. Appropriations for the Job Corps were threatened by the federal budget process on at least four occasions, but the consistent findings from cost-benefit studies, financed by the federal government, that the benefits of Job Corps training exceeded considerably the costs drove the survival and expansion of the program (Cain, 1968; Thornton, Long, and Mallar, 1982). Discussions with early childhood experts have suggested that the survival and expansion of Head Start is largely due to a range of studies on costs and effectiveness, especially the Perry Preschool Evaluation (Barnett 1993, 1996), which showed that benefits far exceeded costs.

But the fact that only about 6 percent of elementary and secondary revenues are derived from the federal government suggests the limits of creating a demand for and supply of cost-effectiveness studies from federal educational programs. Perhaps different strategies need to be used to generate such studies and their uses at state and local levels. Of key importance are the roles of the states; they not only fund a considerable share of education, but they also have a great deal of authority and discretion in guiding local spending. For example, almost all states have established standards and testing for their schools with various interventions, such as incentives for good results and greater state monitoring when the results are poor.

Given the existing lack of interest by those who fund research and evaluation and those who use its findings, these educational activities will not be easy to accomplish. One possibility is to work with major policy brokers like the Education Commission of the States to provide seminars on cost-effectiveness analysis with excellent case studies for legislative and governors' staffs dedicated to education. This approach also needs to be pursued in state departments of education and the U.S. Department of Education. Whether it will change matters is unclear. But without a major increase in the demand for and use of cost-effectiveness results in education, it is unlikely that the field will develop more fully over the coming decades.

Notes

1. For a lengthier treatment of these distinctions, as well as a contrasting description of cost-utility analysis, see Levin and McEwan (2000, Chap. 1).
2. For information on cost-benefit and cost-utility analysis, see Levin and McEwan (2000, Chaps. 7, 8).
3. Clune's work provides powerful evidence of the sparse use of cost-effectiveness studies in education.
4. Paradoxically, the Perry Preschool intervention preceded the launch of Head Start. Yet its findings have been influential for considering the effectiveness of Head Start.

References

Barnett, W. S. "Benefit-Cost Analysis of Preschool Education: Findings from a 25-Year Follow-Up." *American Journal of Orthopsychiatry*, 1993, *63*(4), 500–508.
Barnett, W. S. *Lives in the Balance: Age-27 Benefit-Cost Analysis of the High/Scope Perry Preschool Program.* Ypsilanti, Mich.: High/Scope Press, 1996.
Berk, R. A., and Rossi, P. H. *Thinking About Program Evaluation.* Thousand Oaks, Calif.: Sage, 1990.

Cain, G. *Benefit-Cost Estimates for Job Corps.* Madison: University of Wisconsin, 1968.

Clune, W. H. "Methodological Strength and Policy Usefulness of Published Research on Cost-Effectiveness in Education." Unpublished paper. Madison: Center for Policy Research in Education, University of Wisconsin, 1999.

Coleman, J. S. *Equal Opportunity in the United States.* Washington, D.C.: U.S. Government Printing Office, 1966.

Drummond, M. F., O'Brien, B., Stoddart, G. L., and Torrance, G. W. *Methods for the Economic Evaluation of Health Care Programmes.* (2nd ed.) New York: Oxford University Press, 1997.

Eddy, D. M. "Oregon's Methods: Did Cost-Effectiveness Analysis Fail?" *Journal of the American Medical Association,* 1991, *266*(15), 2135–2141.

Fink, A. *Evaluation for Education and Psychology.* Thousand Oaks, Calif.: Sage, 1995.

Gold, M. R., Siegel, J. E., Russell, L. B., and Weinstein, M. C. *Cost-Effectiveness in Health and Medicine.* New York: Oxford University Press, 1996.

Grissmer, D. "Class Size Effects: Assessing the Evidence, Its Policy Implications, and Future Research Agenda." *Educational Evaluation and Policy Analysis,* 1999, *21*(2), 231–248.

Groccia, J. E., and Miller, J. E. (eds.). *Enhancing Productivity: Administrative Instruction, and Technological Strategies.* New Directions for Higher Education, no. 103. San Francisco: Jossey-Bass, 1998.

Hanushek, E. "The Economics of Schooling: Production and Efficiency in Public Schools." *Journal of Economic Literature,* 1986, *24*(3), 1141–1177.

Hanushek, E. "Assessing the Effects of School Resources on Student Performance: An Update." *Educational Evaluation and Policy Analysis,* 1997, *19*(2), 141–164.

Krueger, A. B. "Economic Considerations and Class Size." Working Paper 447. Princeton, N.J.: Industrial Relations Section, Princeton University, 2000.

Jamison, D. T., Mosley, W. T., Measham, A. R., and Bobadilla, J. L. (eds.). *Disease Control Priorities in Developing Countries.* New York: Oxford University Press, 1993.

Levin, H. M. "Cost-Effectiveness in Evaluation Research." In M. Guttenta and E. Struening (eds.), *Handbook of Evaluation Research* (Vol. 2). Thousand Oaks, Calif.: Sage, 1975.

Levin, H. M. *Cost-Effectiveness.* Thousand Oaks, Calif.: Sage, 1983.

Levin, H. M. "Cost-Effectiveness at Quarter Century." In H. M. Levin (ed.), *Evaluation and Education: At Quarter Century, National Society for the Study of Education.* Chicago: University of Chicago Press, 1991.

Levin, H. M., and Driver, C. "Costs of an Educational Voucher System." *Educational Economics,* 1997, *5*(3), 265–283.

Levin, H. M., Glass, G. V., and Meister, G. "Cost-Effectiveness of Computer-Assisted Instruction." *Evaluation Review,* 1987, *11*(1), 50–72.

Levin, H. M., and McEwan, P. *Cost-Effectiveness Analysis: Methods and Applications.* (2nd ed.) Thousand Oaks, Calif.: Sage, 2000.

Mayer, S. E., and Peterson, P. E. "The Costs and Benefits of School Reform." In S. E. Mayer and P. E. Peterson (eds.), *Learning and Earning.* Washington, D.C.: Brookings Institution, 1999.

Merrill Lynch. *The Book of Knowledge: United States Education and Training.* San Francisco: Merrill Lynch and Co., Global Securities Research and Economics Group, 1999.

Monk, D. H., and King, J. A. "Cost Analysis as a Tool for Education Reform." In S. L. Jacobson and R. Berne (eds.), *Reforming Education: The Emerging Systemic Approach.* Thousand Oaks, Calif.: Corwin Press, 1993.

Patton, M. Q. *Utilization-Focused Evaluation: The New Century Text.* (3rd ed.) Thousand Oaks, Calif.: Sage, 1997.

Popham, W. J. *Educational Evaluation.* (2nd ed.) Englewood Cliffs, N.J.: Prentice Hall, 1988.

Rossi, P. H., Freeman, H. E., and Lipsey, M. W. *Evaluation: A Systematic Approach.* (6th ed.) Thousand Oaks, Calif.: Sage, 1999.

Sax, G. *Principles of Educational and Psychological Measurement and Evaluation.* (3rd ed.) Thousand Oaks, Calif.: Sage, 1989.

Sloan, F. A. (ed.). *Valuing Health Care: Costs, Benefits, and Effectiveness of Pharmaceuticals and Other Medical Technologies.* Cambridge: Cambridge University Press, 1995.

Smith, N. L., and Smith, J. K. "State-Level Evaluation Uses of Cost Analysis: A National Descriptive Survey." In J. S. Catterall (ed.), *Implementation of Challenges for Evaluation.* New Directions for Program Evaluation, no. 26. San Francisco: Jossey-Bass, 1985.

Thornton, C., Long, D., and Mallar, C. *A Comparative Evaluation of Benefits and Costs of Job Corps After 48 Months of Observation.* Princeton, N.J.: Mathematica Policy Research, 1982.

HENRY LEVIN is William Heard Kilpatrick Professor of Economics and Education, Teachers College, Columbia University.

6

State legislatures increasingly are mandating standard-ized tests that students must pass to graduate. This chapter suggests that an evaluative technique, auto-biographical memory research using narrative reports from students, can help teachers enrich instruction and learning.

How Memories of School Experiences Can Enrich Educational Evaluations

David B. Pillemer

Analyses of personal experience in schools have the potential to enrich formal evaluations of educational programs. Empirical studies that have employed an autobiographical memory research paradigm have revealed that students' memory narratives are unexpected, and they are unlikely to have surfaced using conventional evaluation techniques and standard outcomes. Students' memories provide suggestions for pedagogical improvement and innovation. In addition, educational narratives contain a firsthand perspective on students' perceptions of success or failure that could prove to be a valuable complement to more traditional evaluations of performance based on test scores.

Autobiographical memory is a prominent research specialty within academic psychology. New data analysis methods enable researchers and evaluators to go beyond case examples and harness more systematically the lessons contained in autobiographical reports. I will demonstrate their potential applicability to school evaluation projects. Autobiographical memory research can be used to address several policy-related questions:

- How can students' memories enrich educational evaluations?
- What learning processes contribute to successful performance on standardized tests, and how might these processes be enhanced?
- What types of teaching strategies are especially likely to be successful in this regard?
- How do personal experiences in school contribute to academic and life success, broadly defined?

New Directions for Evaluation, no. 90, Summer 2001 © Jossey-Bass, A Publishing Unit of John Wiley & Sons, Inc.

Test Scores Do Not Tell The Whole Story:
A Policy Illustration

Longstanding debate about school accountability intensified in the politically charged election year 2000. Calls for more frequent and more rigorous evaluations of student progress were commonplace, with some political candidates advocating a link between school funding and pupils' performance on standardized tests. In Massachusetts, the debate centered on the Massachusetts Comprehensive Assessment System (MCAS) exam. Students must pass the test by their senior year in order to be awarded a high school diploma.

In September 2000, the *Boston Globe* published several "back-to-school" articles. Some writers focused squarely on the MCAS. Because alarmingly high failure rates were expected, policymakers were looking for ways to prevent an educational disaster. Short-term possibilities included allowing multiple retests and eliminating the hardest questions after the first failed testing.

Educators also developed curricular and pedagogical interventions. Because a majority of Boston sophomores failed the math section, this subject received special emphasis: "With an eye on the tough MCAS exam, Boston school officials are launching a new, $3.7 million assault on one subject that continues to stump students: math" (Vaishnav, 2000, p. B1). The focus shifted from memorization and drill to deeper understanding and explanation. According to an elementary school principal, "They're not being asked, 'What is three times two?' . . . They're given a picture of a six-pack of Coke and asked, 'Can you write a multiplication problem from this?'" (Vaishnav, 2000, p. B3). But the shadow of the MCAS remained the focal point of change. Said one administrator, "The bottom line is if this doesn't show up in results on the MCAS, then we've made the wrong choice" (Vaishnav, 2000, p. B3).

Alongside newspaper coverage of the MCAS were back-to-school articles with a different emphasis. Although teachers cannot escape the long shadow of standardized testing, they do not view test preparation as the only or even necessarily the most important part of school learning. For example, teachers also identify personal relationships with students as a critical component of the educational process. According to one veteran middle school teacher, "I always think, 'Oh, I hope I don't lose my touch.' I believe that first day is critical. You have to win them over immediately to get the ones who don't like school or authority figures." This teacher's "self-imposed rule" focuses on relationships rather than numbers: "I have to learn all the kids' names on the first day by noon" (Coleman, 2000, p. B1).

A similar dichotomy is apparent in the literature on educational evaluation, policy, and practice. Evaluation studies frequently assess student success with general and impersonal measures of achievement, including standardized tests, grades, and graduation rates. Successful students receive high marks and scores, and successful schools produce students who score highly. Qualitative sources of data, such as interviews with students and teachers about their personal school experiences, are viewed as overly subjective and ill suited for quantifiable between-student comparisons.

In contrast, other educators emphasize the critical importance of personal experiences in school settings. Sarason (1993) commented broadly on the potential relevance of school experiences to educational policy: "I'm quite aware of the arguments against using personal experience to prove anything or as a basis for a policy recommendation. But what if there are certain types of personal experiences that are so general, so illuminating, so important that they should not be dismissed on grounds of subjectivity?" (p. 10). Tyack (1999) found that people's descriptions of positive school experiences often focused on interpersonal relationships: "They may have forgotten whatever fad was sweeping education or the teenage culture, but they remembered key relationships, especially with teachers" (p. 68). Case examples presented by Altenbaugh (1998), Carson (1996), and Csikszentmihalyi and McCormack (1986) also highlight the enduring impact of relationships with teachers. Carson (1996) expressed concern that the current emphasis on standardized assessment will direct attention away from the personalized role that teachers play in the educational process: "I worry that many—in the general public, in state legislatures, and within the academy—may confuse simplistic assessment outcomes with quality of teaching. I worry that we as professors may think that the students who make the C's in our courses carry little away, when actually, from their perspectives, their lives may have been changed" (p. 17). Support for the power of personal relationships is not limited to selected cases. Large-scale analyses by Astin (1993) and by Pascarella and Terenzini (1991) also demonstrate the positive impact of frequent student-faculty interactions, including personal contact outside the classroom, on student satisfaction and academic attainment.

Examining students' memories of classroom experiences and school relationships adds value to traditional educational evaluations. School memories carry information that is not tapped by achievement test scores and provide a valuable complement to standard modes of assessment.

Remembering "How You Learned It" Improves Test Performance

Traditional evaluations of student and school success employ measures that tap general, impersonal products of learning: mathematical operations, grammar, facts of world history, or foreign language vocabulary. A middle school math achievement test typically includes questions about long division, simple algebra, or geometry rather than questions about the math teacher's specific comments or words of encouragement, his or her interpersonal manner, or specific classroom contributions of other students.

An emphasis on general learning is consistent with commonly shared educational goals and expectations: "Children and people of all ages go to school in order to learn skills and knowledges that they need for life. They do not go to school in order to acquire a storehouse of temporally dated personal memories" (Tulving, 1983, p. 51).

Conventional wisdom notwithstanding, recent research indicates that memories of particular classroom situations are in fact intricately involved in the learning process and contribute to successful performance on test items. A series of studies by Nuthall and Alton-Lee (1995) challenged the idea that "if a student has learned the relevant knowledge, then selection or recall of correct answers in an achievement test occurs more or less automatically" (p. 186). The researchers observed and recorded social studies and science activities in elementary and middle school classrooms. In addition, a content-specific achievement test was administered three different times: at the beginning of a unit, immediately after it was finished, and again twelve months later. About one week after the two posttests, students were interviewed individually. Rather than simply accepting students' responses at face value, the investigators asked them to describe how they had known or learned the answer to each test item. Surprisingly, students frequently could remember the particular learning episode: "Students reported recalling both the specific classroom experiences from which they learned the answer as well as details of the answer itself" (p. 195). For example, a student knew that mercury was the liquid in a thermometer:

INTERVIEWER: Where did you learn that?
CHILD: Mr. B said, what's in a thermometer? And Tony put up his hand and said it was mercury. And it was right, and since then I have remembered.
INTERVIEWER: What did you think at the time?
CHILD: I thought, you [Tony] have got to be wrong. I thought mercury was sort of a jewel or something like that. Or just a planet.
INTERVIEWER: So you thought he was wrong?
CHILD: Mm. I thought it was ink or water [pp. 195–196].

Another child explained how she knew different types of clouds: "He [the teacher] drew some on the blackboard all red (laugh). He didn't do them in white, he did them all red. He did pigs' tails, big fluffy one, feathery-tailed one, flat layers, and a stormy one. . . . We had to do them on a piece of paper and hand them in. . . . It was on a red piece of paper, but we had to do it in pencil . . . and we had to remember what the clouds were 'cause he would rub it off the board, but he would leave the names" (Nuthall and Alton-Lee, 1995, p. 196).

During the interview following the immediate posttest, students linked about half of their test answers to memories of relevant classroom activities. By the time of the delayed twelve-month posttest, the proportion of references to specific activities had dropped to about one-third, with a predictable increase in reports of deduction or inference. Importantly, remembering the original learning experiences was related to accurate test performance: "There was a consistent pattern of association between recall of classroom experiences and recall of the relevant item answer" (Nuthall and Alton-Lee, 1995, p. 209).

This pattern of results was replicated in a study of college students' performance on exams in psychology lecture courses (Conway and others, 1997). For each test item, students indicated how they knew the answer. When the test occurred immediately after the course ended, some students reported that their answers were cued by memories of a specific classroom episode, such as a specific slide demonstration or a professor's comment. As with studies involving younger students, remembering classroom details was associated with accurate test performance. Students receiving higher grades "were able to engage episodic memory more effectively than their colleagues" (p. 408). When students were retested after twenty-five weeks, specific memories had faded, and a considerable amount of course content became "known" rather than "remembered."

Implications for Educators and Evaluators

Research on students' memories of classroom experiences has important implications for improving educational evaluations. When goals include identifying factors that contribute to successful learning, overall summaries based on test scores should be supplemented with analyses of why students responded in particular ways. Contrary to common wisdom that achievement tests directly tap general conceptual knowledge, students' own explanations suggest that specific classroom episodes linger in memory and provide valuable problem-solving cues. Using memory reports more broadly in evaluation research may yield similar insights about participants' thought processes, motivations, and goals.

Memory research also can inform evaluators' efforts to improve pedagogy. Students use richly detailed memories of specific school activities to cue correct answers to test questions, at least during initial stages of learning. Accordingly, teachers must face the challenge of making their lessons engaging and their classrooms interactive: "The more complex and varied the classroom activities, the more likely they are to produce knowledge structures that are rich in episodic and semantic content" (Nuthall and Alton-Lee, 1995, p. 220). Answers that are accessed initially through their connections to firsthand experience will, over time and with repeated exposure, become general knowledge, retrievable apart from their episodic roots.

I have described Boston educators' responses to students' poor performance on the MCAS. One strategy for improving test scores focuses on active discussions and demonstrations rather than rote learning and drill. Why might these innovations be successful? One possible, if unexpected, mechanism is enhanced memory for relevant classroom episodes. When the image of a six-pack of Coke is used to introduce multiplication or a typology of clouds is depicted in a vivid and engaging fashion, the teacher is providing much more than an entertaining context for learning; he or she is creating a context that will enhance immediate test performance and, ultimately, conceptual mastery. Great teachers present facts in a way that stimulates interest and enriches memory: "If you can begin with a story, an example, a startling statistic, a personal experience, or something that has significant attention-holding appeal, attention will be captured" (Weaver and Cotrell, 1987, p. 62). These salient episodes provide memory anchors for short-term learning, retention, and successful immediate test performance. As information is activated repeatedly in new and differing contexts, it loses its dependence on specific memory; it becomes known rather than remembered.

Memories of College

Detailed memories of particular classroom episodes provide mental links to correct test answers. Students who successfully engage episodic memory while taking an exam do better than students who fail to do so. But the value of school memories is not limited to strengthening students' test performance. Systematic analyses of memory narratives also reveal broader, pedagogically and policy-relevant insights about students' well-being and school success.

My colleagues and I have conducted an extensive series of questionnaire studies examining memories of college. In initial studies (Pillemer, Rhinehart, and White, 1986), undergraduates attending Wellesley and Harvard reported the first four memories to come to mind of their first year in college and then rated the memories on scales of emotionality and life impact. Several clear data patterns were apparent. Most of the remembered events were specific and were rated as at least moderately emotional. Content analyses indicated that the memories frequently described social activities—only about 20 percent focused squarely on academics—and centrally involved other people. Temporal distributions based on participants' estimates of when in the academic year the remembered events had occurred showed a marked peak at the point of transition into college: approximately 30 percent of all first-year memories fell in September.

These patterns were replicated in studies involving Wellesley alumnae who had graduated two, twelve, or twenty-two years earlier (Pillemer, Goldsmith, Panter, and White, 1988). A majority of memories described specific episodes, although specificity declined with increasing time since graduation. The narratives were rich in emotional and interpersonal content, with about one-quarter of the memories targeting academics explicitly. The temporal distribution of memories for each of the three alumnae groups showed a sharp peak in September, with approximately 40 percent of all first-year memories falling into this brief transitional period.

In follow-up studies, Wellesley undergraduates and alumnae were asked to describe "influential" college experiences rather than to report the first memories to come to mind (Pillemer, Picariello, Law, and Reichman, 1996). Again, undergraduate students' memories of their first year in college frequently described specific events, they were rated as strongly emotional, and a majority focused on nonacademic themes. The temporal distribution of memories showed a sharp peak at the beginning of the school year, with 32 percent of remembered events occurring in September. Alumnae who had graduated one, eleven, or twenty-one years earlier were not asked to limit their responses to first-year memories; they were asked to recount influential events that had occurred at any point in their four college years. Nevertheless, a similar pattern of results was apparent. A majority of memories involved specific episodes, and the remembered events were rated as strongly emotional. The proportion of distinctly academic memories was 43 percent. The temporal distribution of memories peaked at the beginning of the first college year, with 25 percent of datable influential events from all four years occurring in the first three months of college. A smaller peak was apparent at the other major transition point, the end of senior year; 10 percent of all remembered influential events occurred in the last two months of college.

More Implications for Educators and Evaluators

How might school memories inform educational evaluations and policies? The findings provide systematic support for the idea that the impact of schooling is not limited to impersonal learning of general knowledge contained in textbooks. Former students vividly remember specific, highly emotional, interpersonal events for years following graduation, and they judge those events to be influential in shaping their lives. The memories serve a directive function (Pillemer, 1998). They come to mind frequently, and they continue to provide guidance long after the initial transitory encounter.

Critical Beginnings. Although educational evaluations emphasize end products—achievement test scores, final grades, and graduation rates— temporal distributions of memories reshift the focus to beginnings and, more generally, significant points of life transition. The start of a new school experience is important not only as a staging area for substantive work to follow; it is itself a key educational juncture. During times of transition, students lack a general understanding of how to succeed in the new environment, and they may feel unsure and vulnerable. They may be especially receptive to and influenced by specific events at such times. Salient "educational episodes"—an illuminating classroom activity, an enlightening conversation with a fellow student, a humiliating failure—provide initial guidance about how to achieve success and avoid trouble (Pillemer, 1998; Pillemer, Picariello, Law, and Reichman, 1996). A teacher's intuition that first impressions are strongly related to success in the classroom, described earlier, is consistent with temporal patterns found in memory studies. The teacher stated that the "first day is critical" and that she had to "win them over immediately to get the ones who don't like school or authority figures." When I have shared the results of our studies with teaching colleagues, they often express surprise and even anxiety. The common views that school exerts its impact primarily by fostering the gradual acquisition of abstract concepts and that a teacher has a broad time window within which to reach students should be modified to include special pedagogical concern for resonant classroom episodes and thoughtful classroom planning for critical points of transition.

Improving Pedagogy. Pillemer, Picariello, Law, and Reichman (1996) provide several illustrations of how students' memories of interactions with teachers may inform pedagogy. Although the examples come from college settings, the lessons do not appear to be limited to older students. And the strategy of collecting and analyzing students' firsthand accounts of classroom process can be used to inform practice at all educational levels.

A first issue is how to give corrective feedback to students, a topic that is especially important in the light of increasingly urgent calls for more stringent standards. Students' reactions to negative evaluations appear to depend in large part on how the feedback is administered. Surprising and inadequately explained criticism may lead to lower self-esteem, anger, and distancing. One former student remembered a stiff rebuke:

> In my sophomore year, I took an English literature course. I loved the course material, enjoyed writing papers, and felt pretty good about it until . . . I wrote an essay on my interpretation of a poem. I felt I had great insight into a special meaning within the verse. When the paper was returned, the teacher told me I didn't have any understanding of the material and she hoped I wasn't going to be an English major. I remember her pinched face and small, tight mouth as she said these things to me. I thought no way do I want to be like her. So I changed my major from English to Sociology [Pillemer, Picariello, Law, and Reichman, 1996, p. 333].

A participant in Altenbaugh's (1998) interview study of high school dropouts felt humiliated and devalued by the teacher's public reporting of test grades:

> Every time after a test . . . she would pass out the tests and read out your scores. The perfect students would be read off first, and there would be like three A's in the class, everybody else are D's and failed. I guess the teacher did that to make the people embarrassed and to make them try harder [p. 58].

Teachers' criticism need not have a demoralizing and undermining effect. Strongly negative feedback can be inspirational if the student is given thoughtful guidance and an opportunity to do better—for example:

After a terrible 1st year academically, my second year I really began to apply myself. Still, even though I wanted to do well I had this feeling that I didn't belong at Wellesley; I felt like I was not "smart enough" to be there and compete. Then, after studying for my [politics] exam for days, I did terribly on it. My self-confidence was virtually nonexistent. My professor had written a note on my exam to go talk to him about my grade and I did. He spent an hour going over my exam, showing me how to take an essay exam, and in the end he let me take my exam over. After a string of C's, I never received one again. In fact my G.P.A. [grade point average] went from 2.2 my first semester to 3.89 my last. That one hour in my [politics] professor's office had to be [my] most influential experience at Wellesley [Pillemer, Picariello, Law, and Reichman, 1996, p. 334].

A related classroom management issue involves the timing of critical feedback. Students entering new environments are highly attentive to and influenced by even casual input from powerful or respected others—for example:

My first writing assignment—freshman year—a description. I described the autumn foliage. The comment I got back—"too kodachrome"—puzzled me. The colors *were* kodachrome, to me. . . . Perhaps I remembered this because it was part of the process of jettisoning hope and trust and opting for survival which characterized my first months there [Pillemer, Picariello, Law, and Reichman, 1996, p. 334].

The teacher's relatively innocuous statement attained special significance in part because the beginning student lacked a firm intellectual and emotional foundation. The implication for educators is not to eliminate critical feedback but rather to temper, clarify, and support that feedback during the uncertainty of transitional periods. Faced with the knowledge that new students frequently are vulnerable to overreaction and misunderstanding, teachers should finely tune their feedback to fit students' cognitive and emotional timetables.

A third pedagogical issue involves personal connections linking students and teachers. Student-teacher interactions are represented prominently in academic memories. The personal linkage infuses impersonal learning with affective meaning. Students want to learn because their teachers are people whom they wish to emulate: "The main function of the teacher . . . is to make being an adult seem like a worthwhile option" (Csikszentmihalyi, 1997, p. 80)—for example:

My teacher was . . . something of a tyrant. . . . Nonetheless, [the professor] and I got along fine. She gave me B's; I worked my tail off for them. When I came back from my summer abroad, she took me out to lunch with her. . . . The fact that she found my off-campus life—my summer—of great interest and import meant a lot to me, and I've not forgotten our lunch. I went on to major in [her area of study], partly because of her attention to me [Pillemer, Picariello, Law, and Reichman, 1996, p. 335].

Even a relatively superficial personal connection may prove to be motivational. A Wellesley student's decision to major in biochemistry rather than biology was influenced by a teacher's relatively modest efforts to be connected:

I didn't go to any bio office hours, but I went to her [chemistry professor's] office hours, not very much, more like twice and she knew my name. But it was an intro class and I didn't really expect that, so that was like, you know, an encouraging sign . . . and just very enthusiastic about chemistry [Pillemer, Picariello, Law, and Reichman, 1996, p. 335].

The middle school teacher who was quoted earlier in this chapter felt that she must "learn all the kids' names on the first day by noon" in an effort to "win them over immediately." Once a personal relationship is established, learning is fueled by the power of human connection.

In contrast, memories of strong, positive bonds between teachers and students are largely missing in the school narratives told by former high school dropouts (Altenbaugh, 1998): "Students entered a large and intimidating high school facility and encountered impersonal, if not hostile, instructors. A social and intellectual gulf existed between teachers and students, and this contributed to school leaving. . . . Success or failure, as these school leavers saw it, was based strictly on their relationships with teachers, and this gives the process of learning a high level of subjective meaning. . . . More than alienation from academic subject matter, . . . students felt estranged from the adults who were supposed to help them" (p. 69). Students who are struggling to succeed or survive in school apparently need more than increasingly stringent academic standards and formal tests; they need pedagogical interventions that enhance human connections with teachers.

Using School Memories as an Evaluative Marker

School memories not only provide suggestions for pedagogical improvement; they also contain students' firsthand evaluations of their own success or failure. The impact of schooling is not captured fully by grade point averages and test scores. Each student also carries away the products of personal school experiences, represented in vivid recollections. The memories are not static, passive records of school events, residing outside conscious awareness. Memories of salient educational episodes come to mind repeatedly; they are active, persistent influences on self-concept and life decisions (Pillemer, 1998). The belief system that a student constructs about life in school becomes part of his or her intellectual road map: "A life is not 'how it was' but how it is interpreted and reinterpreted, told and retold" (Bruner, 1987, p. 31). In this sense, students' school narratives provide educators and evaluators with essential information about how school was experienced, how it has come to be understood, and how it continues to direct the life course.

What types of memories represent successful educational outcomes? It should be possible to specify qualities associated with definitions of success and to observe whether these qualities are represented in students' narratives. One potential indicator is the incidence of memories of positive originating events (Pillemer, 1998): episodes in which a student is inspired to achieve a respected and fulfilling goal. Most educators would agree that schools should do more than transmit factual information; they should help students construct worthwhile goals and inspire a persistent motivation to achieve them.

People frequently trace the beginnings of a particular life pursuit to a memorable originating event. For example, photographer Margaret Bourke-White was inspired by a childhood memory:

> Father . . . took me with him on trips to factories where he was supervising the setting up of his presses. One day . . . I saw a foundry for the first time. I remember climbing with him to a sooty balcony and looking down into the mysterious depths below. "Wait," Father said, and then in a rush the blackness was broken by a sudden magic of flowing metal and flying sparks. I can hardly describe my joy. . . . Later when I became a photographer . . . this memory was so vivid and so alive that it shaped the whole course of my career [Bourke-White, 1992, p. 425].

Although the event did not take place in a school setting, teachers may ignite a similar passion by exposing students to engaging real-world experiences.

Two additional positive examples took place in college classrooms:

> In my first Philosophy class . . . I remember a discussion on a moral dilemma concerning a woman and two children. The woman was taking care of a friend's child and her own child while at an outing by a lake. The children are out on a canoe which capsizes, both children are drowning. The dilemma was: which child should she save? [The professor] was very eloquent on the subject and it seemed like everyone in the class was talking. . . . It was very much a sensory as well as intellectual experience and was the class which made me become a Philosophy Major [Pillemer, 1998, p. 73].

> I don't remember the *exact* material, except that it was Egyptian art. . . . She was an *amazing* lecturer—super excited about the subject, talking non-stop, and racing back and forth across the stage. The time went very quickly. . . . [The professor] had gotten me so excited about art history,

that I left the auditorium absolutely positive that art history was my calling in life [Pillemer, 1998, p. 73].

McAdams and others (1999) identified two additional memory categories that may reflect educational success or failure. Some narratives contain redemption stories, whereas others portray the theme of contamination. In a *redemption* story, a negative episode has a positive long-term impact. In a *contamination* story, an initially positive experience has a negative ultimate outcome. An example of a contamination story is the memory, described previously, in which a student's enjoyment of English literature was dashed by her professor's stern and surprising assessment that she was unsuited for that area of study. Redemption is illustrated by the memory of poor academic performance in a politics class being overcome by the professor's careful one-on-one interaction and the student's subsequent high achievement.

Redemption carries the worldview that adversity is surmountable: the person "is interpreting past difficulties and challenges in such a way as to conclude that good things can come from very bad events. . . . Such a story suggests hope and progress in life and may thus confer upon the storyteller a general coping advantage in life" (McAdams and others, 1999). In contrast, contamination reflects the belief that even promising beginnings will be spoiled: "People who see the past as good turning into bad are less optimistic about the present and the future for their own lives and are less able to commit themselves to improving the lives of others in the present and the future" (McAdams and others, 1999). In fact, people who frame their pasts in terms of redemption show evidence of psychological well-being, but people who see their lives through the lens of contamination are more likely to experience maladjustment (McAdams and others, 1999).

In successful classrooms and schools, redemption rather than contamination stories should be strongly represented in students' educational narratives. Teachers, administrators, and parents can help students mentally frame their accomplishments or shortcomings in a way that encourages hope rather than apathy. Strong criticism need not imply a negative evaluation of a student's underlying capabilities. A more beneficial and forward-looking message is that criticism is given because adults have positive long-term expectations for the student's ultimate success and are eager to invest in that success.

Conclusion

The lessons for both educators and evaluators contained in personal narratives of school experiences would not be uncovered by standard measures of academic achievement. They capture a different but still vitally important aspect of learning—what has been called "autobiographical intelligence"

(Pillemer, 1998). Successful students know more than the answers to test questions; they also know how to pursue long-term goals, avoid pitfalls, and remain motivated. These qualities are constructed in part through personal interactions with teachers, and they are captured and energized by vivid and persistent memories. Memory narratives offer evaluators a rich and relatively untapped source of information about students, teaching, and educational effectiveness.

References

Altenbaugh, R. J. "'Some Teachers Are Ignorant': Teachers and Teaching Through Urban School Leavers' Eyes." In B. M. Franklyn (ed.), *When Children Don't Learn: Student Failure and the Culture of Teaching.* New York: Teachers College Press, 1998.

Astin, A. W. *What Matters in College: Four Critical Years Revisited.* San Francisco: Jossey-Bass, 1993.

Bourke-White, M. "Portrait of Myself." In J. K. Conway (ed.), *Written by Herself.* New York: Vintage, 1992.

Bruner, J. S. "Life as Narrative." *Social Research,* 1987, *54,* 11–32.

Carson, B. H. "Thirty Years of Stories: The Professor's Place in Student Memories." *Change,* 1996, *28,* 11–17.

Coleman, S. "First-Day Jitters." *Boston Globe,* Sept. 6, 2000, pp. B1, B6.

Conway, M. A., and others. "Changes in Memory Awareness During Learning: The Acquisition of Knowledge by Psychology Undergraduates." *Journal of Experimental Psychology: General,* 1997, *126,* 393–413.

Csikszentmihalyi, M. "Intrinsic Motivation and Effective Teaching: A Flow Analysis." In J. L. Bess (ed.), *Teaching Well and Liking It: Motivating Faculty to Teach Effectively.* Baltimore, Md.: Johns Hopkins University Press, 1997.

Csikszentmihalyi, M., and McCormack, J. "The Influence of Teachers." *Phi Delta Kappan,* Feb. 1986, pp. 415–419.

McAdams, D. P., and others. "When Bad Things Turn Good and Good Things Turn Bad: Sequences of Redemption and Contamination in Life Narratives and Their Relation to Psychosocial Adaptation in Midlife Adults and in Students." Unpublished manuscript, 1999.

Nuthall, G., and Alton-Lee, A. "Assessing Classroom Learning: How Students Use Their Knowledge and Experience to Answer Classroom Achievement Test Questions in Science and Social Studies." *American Educational Research Journal,* 1995, *32,* 185–223.

Pascarella, E. T., and Terenzini, P. T. *How College Affects Students.* San Francisco: Jossey-Bass, 1991.

Pillemer, D. B. *Momentous Events, Vivid Memories.* Cambridge, Mass.: Harvard University Press, 1998.

Pillemer, D. B., Goldsmith, L. R., Panter, A. T., and White, S. H. "Very Long-Term Memories of the First Year in College." *Journal of Experimental Psychology: Learning, Memory, and Cognition,* 1988, *14,* 709–715.

Pillemer, D. B., Picariello, M. L., Law, A. B., and Reichman, J. S. "Memories of College: The Importance of Specific Educational Episodes." In D. C. Rubin (ed.), *Remembering Our Past: Studies in Autobiographical Memory.* New York: Cambridge University Press, 1996.

Pillemer, D. B., Rhinehart, E. D., and White, S. H. "Memories of Life Transitions: The First Year in College." *Human Learning,* 1986, *5,* 109–123.

Sarason, S. B. *The Case for Change: Rethinking the Preparation of Educators.* San Francisco: Jossey-Bass, 1993.

Tulving, E. *Elements of Episodic Memory.* New York: Oxford University Press, 1983.

Tyack, D. "Needed: More Educational Conservationists." *Education Week,* June 23, 1999,
    p. 68.
Vaishnav, A. "New Initiative Aims to Make Math More Than Just Numbers." *Boston
    Globe,* Sept. 12, 2000, pp. B1, B3.
Weaver, R. L., II, and Cotrell, H. W. "Lecturing: Essential Communication Strategies."
    In M. G. Weimer (ed.), *Teaching Large Classes Well.* New Directions for Teaching and
    Learning, no. 32. San Francisco: Jossey-Bass, 1987.

*DAVID B. PILLEMER is the William R. Kenan, Jr., Professor of Psychology, Welles-
ley College.*

7

*Case studies from three cities show how concrete evidence
often runs counter to a common wisdom. Using the example of professional development for teachers, this chapter
illustrates how evaluation evidence can offer insights into
education policies.*

Large-Scale Professional Development for Schoolteachers: Cases from Pittsburgh, New York City, and the National School Reform Faculty

Edward Miech, Bill Nave, Frederick Mosteller

Professional development for schoolteachers in the United States represents a
massive investment of resources in efforts to improve schooling. In elementary
and secondary education, policymakers and administrators largely rely on professional development to keep their experienced teachers up-to-date in subject matter knowledge, methods of planning and presenting lessons, issues of
early childhood and adolescent development, and changes in school-related
laws, policies, and practices.

Professional development for schoolteachers—also called staff development and in-service education—encompasses many shapes and forms. University course work is a popular part of the professional development
repertoire. Also common in the repertoire is the one-afternoon workshop, typically held in an auditorium or other meeting space on the school grounds for
an hour or two after the students have gone home. An invited speaker usually addresses a large group of schoolteachers, talking about an issue related
to children, classrooms, or schools. As a one-shot workshop, the goal of this
type of professional development is to increase teachers' knowledge of a par-

This research was supported in part by a grant from the Andrew W. Mellon Foundation
to the American Academy of Arts and Sciences project *Initiatives for Children* for its Center for Evaluation. We also appreciate the helpful suggestions of John Emerson, Lincoln
Moses, Marjorie Olson, Jessa Piaia, Cleo Youtz, and Richard Light. Special thanks go to
the Ford Foundation for permission to use material from their archives and to archivist
Alan Divack for his assistance.

ticular topic, with the hope that this new knowledge will somehow translate into change in classrooms and improved student achievement. The general effectiveness of this kind of one-afternoon workshop, when measured in formal evaluations, is consistently very low (Moore-Johnson, 1990; Nave, 2000b), suggesting that its popularity as a model of professional development may be more for administrative convenience than for educational efficacy.

This chapter considers three examples of ambitious, large-scale professional development programs—in Pittsburgh, in New York City, and a National School Reform Faculty (NSRF) program—that contrast sharply with the one-shot workshop and the "night school" model and reviews some surprising findings associated with evaluations of those initiatives.

In the case of Pittsburgh, an urban school district gave all of its high school teachers an eight-week mini-sabbatical during the school year to upgrade their skills and knowledge in a special teacher center based in a fully operational inner-city high school staffed by master teachers. As part of the elaborate design, fifty specially trained substitutes took over instructional responsibilities for each cohort of participating teachers and department heads during their eight-week professional development experience at the Schenley High School Teacher Center. One of the surprises of the Pittsburgh initiative, which relied primarily on formative evaluation, was that an ambitious, large-scale, and systematic program could be so comprehensively implemented in a school district. Over a four-year period, over 925 high school teachers in the Pittsburgh public schools took part in the mini-sabbatical, representing a remarkable participation rate of 98 percent.

In New York City, the 22,000-student public school district known as Community District Two integrated an ambitious professional development initiative into a systemic process for improving instruction in its elementary and junior high schools. The four basic components of the district-wide professional development program consisted of a professional development laboratory (based loosely on Pittsburgh's Schenley High School Teacher Center), instructional consulting services, peer visits by school principals and schoolteachers to observe excellent instructional practices, and home-grown teacher institutes (Elmore and Burney, 1998). As part of its evaluation strategy, District Two employed direct observation on the part of its senior administrators. The deputy superintendent and director of professional development spent at least two days each week at schools to evaluate the quality and progress of on-site instruction, and the superintendent visited each school at least once a year. A surprising finding from these direct observational evaluations was that these senior administrators deemed it necessary to replace two-thirds of the principals in the district over a four-year period and that principals found it necessary to replace over half of all teachers in the district over an eight-year period.

The third case is the NSRF program sponsored by the Annenberg Institute for School Reform. This professional development initiative, involving hundreds of schools across the United States, creates small, on-site groups of teachers led by a "coach"—typically a specially trained peer—who meet regularly to discuss ways to improve their teaching practice. The Annenberg Institute retained one of us (Bill Nave) to design and conduct a formal evaluation of the program, and a surprising finding from the theory-based evaluation was that several teachers changed their classroom teaching practice dramatically without being aware of it. This finding departs from the conventional wisdom in the professional development literature that schoolteachers must become more reflective about their practice before they can make changes in their teaching (Nave, 2000b).

Schenley High School Teacher Center

The Pittsburgh Public Schools hired a new superintendent, Dr. Richard C. Wallace, at the close of the tumultuous 1970s. Difficulties surrounding the creation of a school desegregation plan acceptable to the Pennsylvania Human Rights Commission had led to large decreases in enrollment in Pittsburgh's public schools as parents enrolled their children in the city's Catholic parochial schools and other private schools. By 1980, the Pittsburgh Public Schools enrolled only 47,000 students, down by about a third from 70,000 students in 1970 (Wallace, 1996).

During the 1981–1982 school year, Wallace selected a small committee of teachers and administrators to conduct a feasibility study on the creation of a teacher center modeled after the ideas of a teaching hospital. The center would be housed at an operating high school, and teachers would learn new instructional skills in the setting of actual classrooms with actual students.

Wallace developed a set of committees involving hundreds of teachers and others in Pittsburgh to create a detailed design for the teacher center (Report to the Ford Foundation VI, 1987). The plan emerging from the committees called for the teacher center to be housed in an existing comprehensive high school and to host groups of about fifty "visiting teachers" for eight-week mini-sabbaticals at the center. A specially trained cadre of fifty replacement teachers would take over the instructional responsibilities of the visiting teachers while they were at the center. The center's four goals were (1) to improve instruction, (2) upgrade teachers' content knowledge, (3) improve teachers' understanding of adolescent development in relation to effective teaching, and (4) provide a professional growth experience for teachers (Teacher Center Proposal to Ford Foundation, 1982).

The teacher center's goal of improving instruction was to be accomplished by training teachers to use Madeline Hunter's (1982) model of mastery teaching. Teachers would learn about the model in seminars, then watch it demonstrated by the resident teachers. Next, they would try it while being observed and then receive feedback on their attempts at the new practice. Wallace called this process the "clinical teaching experience" (Wallace and others, 1984).

Wallace selected Schenley High School to host the teacher center for several reasons, including it was slated to close due to declining enrollment and because it ranked last academically among the city's twelve remaining high schools (Wallace, 1996). To Schenley's health careers magnet program

Wallace added two new magnet programs—technology and international studies—and installed the International Baccalaureate program (Report to the Ford Foundation I, 1983; Report to the Ford Foundation VI, 1987). He hoped that these three additional programs would attract talented high school students to enroll at Schenley (Wallace, 1996).

Wallace negotiated with the Pittsburgh Federation of Teachers to waive some contract provisions and to close Schenley on paper, then reopen it with a resident faculty member selected from among the best teachers in the city (Memorandum of Understanding, 1982; Report to the Ford Foundation I, 1983). The union agreed to a similar process for selecting the fifty replacement teachers (Wallace, 1996). The district's professional development team trained the new Schenley resident teachers in clinical teaching experience skills during the summer of 1983. When the Schenley High School Teacher Center opened that fall, it hosted the fifty replacement teachers as the first group to be trained in those skills at the center (Wallace and others, 1984).

The second and third groups of visiting teachers included the department chairs from the other eleven high schools. Wallace insisted they be among the first to experience the training at Schenley to set a positive example for teachers in their departments (Wallace, 1996).

Daily Operation of the Schenley High School Teacher Center. The operation of the teacher center was complex. An efficient way to describe its operation is to follow "Chris," a hypothetical high school math teacher in Pittsburgh.[2] During the week prior to Chris's eight weeks at the Teacher Center, the Schenley resident teacher who will be his mentor meets with him to plan for a smooth transition. Together they plan the curriculum that the replacement teacher will cover while Chris is at Schenley, and Chris introduces the replacement teacher to students.

The clinical teaching episode is the centerpiece of Chris's Schenley experience (Davis, 1986). During the second week at Schenley, he plans a lesson for one of the resident teacher's classes using skills emphasized by the clinical teaching experience. He makes these plans jointly with the host resident teacher and the paired visiting teacher. A team of at least six peers observes his lesson, taking verbatim notes throughout the lesson.

Immediately after the lesson, Chris writes a reflection on the lesson, noting how the clinical teaching experience methods worked or failed to work and what he might do differently next time. At the same time, the observers meet to organize their notes into clinical teaching experience categories and discuss their feedback for him. Within twenty-four hours of the lesson, Chris meets with the group, offers personal reflections on the lesson, and listens to the group's critique of the lesson. He experiences about a dozen of these clinical teaching episodes during the middle six weeks of the eight weeks at Schenley.

During these middle six weeks, Chris also continues to attend seminars on adolescent development and math teaching, and in addition participates in a special project of his own choosing. He also meets periodically with the replacement teacher who is covering his classes to review what the students are doing.

During the eighth week at Schenley, Chris spends much time planning for the transition back to the home school and his math classes. He also works with the mentor, principal, and department chair to refine follow-up plans for continued professional growth.

Results of the Schenley High School Teacher Center. Finally, it became time to evaluate the impact of the Schenley process.

Evaluation Evidence for Changes in Teachers' Instructional Behaviors. A research team from the University of Pittsburgh asked a group of randomly selected special education teachers to volunteer for a study of the influence of the Schenley experience on their instructional behaviors. Twelve teachers from this randomly selected group volunteered to participate in the study. The researchers observed their classes both before and after their eight weeks at Schenley, noting the behaviors of both teachers and students. The researchers concluded that some effective teaching behaviors increased in frequency after the teachers' time at Schenley (Zigmond, Kohnke, and Miller, 1986):

Direct instruction increased from an average of 19 percent of a class period to an average of 32 percent.

Teachers used behavioral objectives to introduce instructional tasks 20 percent more of the time.

Time spent on behavior management decreased from an average of 4 percent of class time to an average of 2 percent.

Student on-task behavior increased from an average of 61 percent of class time to an average of 78 percent.

Evaluation Evidence for Changes in Student Achievement. Researchers have presented evidence for increases in standardized test scores after the Schenley Teacher Center opened, both at Schenley and across the district. For example, Table 7.1 shows gains from 1983 to 1984 in the percentage of students scoring at or above the national median in each of five high school subjects. The average increase for all five subjects in the percentage of students scoring at or above the median at Schenley was 23.4 percentage points, and the average increase for the district was 7.6 percentage points. Schenley scores moved from last to the top half of all high schools in three of the subjects tested (Report to the Ford Foundation III, 1984).

Table 7.2 shows that the average increase across the five subjects (weighted equally) in the percentage of Schenley students at or above the national norm from 1983 to 1986 was 27 percentage points (Report to the Ford Foundation VI, 1987).

Enrollment Changes in Pittsburgh Public Schools. The opening of the Schenley High School Teacher Center heralded other changes in Pittsburgh's schools. By the mid-1980s, over a thousand students per year were reenrolling in the public schools, and by 1992, all schools that had been closed during the 1970s and early 1980s had reopened. In addition, Pittsburgh had to lease space from closed Catholic schools to accommodate the enrollment

**Table 7.1. Percentage of Students at or Above the National Median
in Five Subjects, 1983–1984**

Schenley High School District

	1983	1984	1983	1984
Reading	28	37	45	49
Language	27	58	45	56
Algebra I	29	73	57	66
Physical science	21	47	32	39
Social science	31	38	49	56

growth (Wallace, 1996). These reenrollment numbers satisfied the targets in the district desegregation plan.

Teachers' Experience After Schenley. Reports from survey responses of teachers suggested difficulty for teachers back at their home schools after they completed their Schenley experience. Teachers found the observations and feedback on their teaching less helpful than it had been at Schenley because the department chairs, principals, and assistant principals doing the observations and providing the feedback were less skilled in this process than the Schenley resident teachers had been. Survey responses also suggested that teachers found it challenging to secure the time to carry out their follow-up professional growth plans at their home schools. The organization and culture of their home schools was not as conducive as Schenley had been in supporting their continued professional growth (Report to the Ford Foundation III, 1984).

Schenley Phase Two. After nearly all of Pittsburgh's high school teachers had experienced their eight-week sessions at Schenley during its initial four years of operation, a committee appointed by Wallace decided to keep the Teacher Center open with a slightly modified purpose. During this second phase of the Teacher Center, Schenley would host high school teachers new to Pittsburgh who had not been among the original groups of visiting teachers. Schenley would also host groups of visiting teachers from high schools in neighboring districts, which paid tuition for their teachers to attend (Report to the Ford Foundation VII, 1989).

New York City, Community District Two

Anthony Alvarado became superintendent of District Two in 1987 following eighteen months as chancellor of the New York City schools.[3] Before that, he had been superintendent for ten years in New York's District Four, comprising Spanish Harlem in upper Manhattan. While he led District Four, Alvarado encouraged teachers and administrators to be creative in developing programs that would support student success in a district where academic success for students was not common. The much-studied Central Park East Elementary and Secondary Schools, founded by Deborah Meier, are

**Table 7.2. Percentage of Schenley Students at or Above
the National Median, 1983–1986**

	1983	1984	1985	1986
Reading	28	37	45	46
Language	27	58	61	66
Algebra I	29	73	68	50
Algebra II	44	44	65	66
Physical science	21	47	71	58

examples of creative programs initiated in District Four when Alvarado was superintendent there (Elmore and Burney, 1998).

District Two is one of thirty-two local community districts in New York City created in the late 1960s as a result of political pressure to decentralize the schools and allow neighborhood control of neighborhood schools (grades K-8 only; high schools are still under city-wide jurisdiction). District Two in Manhattan includes the East Side of Central Park south of Ninety-Sixth Street, crossing at Fifty-Ninth Street to include all of Manhattan south of the park except for one part of the Lower East Side, which is Community District One (Elmore and Burney, 1998).

District Two has twenty-four elementary schools, seven junior high schools, and seventeen option schools (alternative schools of choice with various grade-level patterns), for a total of forty-eight. It has twenty-two thousand students (29 percent white, 14 percent African American, 22 percent Latino, 34 percent Asian, and less than 1 percent Native American) and about a thousand teachers. Recent immigrants come from over one hundred countries; 20 percent of students use English as their second language. Half of the students come from families below the poverty line; two thousand (9 percent) are special education students (Elmore and Burney, 1998).

Using professional development as a systemwide process for improving instruction is in part a reaction to Alvarado's earlier experience as superintendent in District Four. His strategy of supporting the development of creative programs transformed some schools in the district (most notable Deborah Meier's Central Park East Schools) but did not change all the schools in the district. Desiring to improve learning for all students in District Two, Alvarado created a strategy of using professional development district-wide to focus tightly on instructional improvement in every classroom. He began with an emphasis on literacy instruction not only because it made sense in terms of the needs of the district's students, but also because he believed that improvements in literacy would show up in the results of the city's annual standardized test, the California Test of Basic Skills (CTBS) (Elmore and Burney, 1998).

Alvarado's strategy of focusing professional development tightly on improvement of instruction district-wide involved every educator in the district. He held principals accountable for the improvement of instruction in their schools, evaluating them annually based on their plan for deployment of resources and activities for teachers (Elmore and Burney, 1998).

Operation of District Two's Professional Development Program. Most of the activities for teacher improvement in District Two take the form of one of the following four models or activities (Elmore and Burney, 1998).

• *The Professional Development Laboratory.* According to Bea Johnstone, District Two director of professional development, the idea grew out of a visit she and some parents and teachers made to the Phase Two Schenley High School Teacher Center in Pittsburgh during the 1980s (Elmore and Burney, 1998). Each year staff members responsible for teacher training in District Two designate some experienced teachers as resident teachers. Other teachers in the district apply to become visiting teachers, who spend three weeks observing and practicing in a resident teacher's classroom.

In a typical year, sixteen to twenty visiting teachers receive this training (the system is not used at full capacity because resident teachers do not accept visiting teachers during each cycle). District Two, New York University, and the United Federation of Teachers established the professional development laboratory in 1991 with support from the Morgan Foundation.

• *Instructional consulting services.* Outside consultants and district consultants work with individual teachers and groups of teachers at a school site.

• *Intervisitations and peer networks.* Occurring both within and outside the district, these are designed to bring principals and teachers into contact with exemplary practices. Principals usually initiate visits outside the district and bring their teachers to the site, in preparation for developing a new teaching practice back at their home school. Intervisitations and peer consultations are a routine part of district life (the district budgets three hundred days per year for the work).

• *Off-site training.* This typically occurs at summer institutes hosted by the district. Topics for these institutes emerge from local school planning for the next year's professional development focus.

Results of District Two's Professional Development. All students in New York City take the CTBS annually. One way to look at student performance is to examine District Two's rank in the aggregate academic performance of its students. During Alvarado's tenure in the district, its ranking among the city's thirty-two districts moved from sixteenth (which would be expected based on its students' socioeconomic status, half of them living below the poverty line) to second in aggregate performance of reading and math (Elmore and Burney, 1998).

Another way to analyze student performance is to compare the CTBS reading scores of students in the district to the average scores of students across New York City. Table 7.3 shows the proportion of District 2 students in the top and bottom quarter of reading test scores compared to the city average (Elmore and Burney, 1998).[4]

Table 7.3. District Two California Test of Basic Skills,
Reading Score Distribution

	Students Scoring in Bottom Quarter	Students Scoring in Top Quarter
District Two	11%	40%
New York City	24	18
United States	25	25

Scores from the spring 1997 CTBS reading test showed that citywide, 24 percent of students scored in the lowest quarter, while only 11 percent of District Two students scored in the bottom quarter. At the top of the scale, only 18 percent of students citywide scored in the highest quarter, while 40 percent of District Two students scored in the top quarter (Elmore and Burney, 1998).

National School Reform Faculty

The professional development specialists at the Annenberg Institute for School Reform launched the NSRF program during the summer of 1995. They designed the program based on two factors:

The recently published research of McLaughlin and Talbert (1990, 1993) suggesting a relationship between the degree of collegiality among members of high school academic departments and improved teaching and student achievement

Input from teachers in the field requesting ongoing professional development at their own schools in addition to summer-only workshops

The NSRF developers invited schools to create small groups of teachers of four to ten members to become a "Critical Friends Group" (CFG) and to select one of their number (or a trusted outsider) to become their coach. During a six-day summer session, the Annenberg professional developers trained the coach in the skills needed to create and sustain a high degree of collegiality among the CFG members. Among the skills the coaches learn is how to use a set of structured conversations, or protocols, that keep the members focused on the analysis of the work at hand—for example, a sample of student writing—in an objective and nonjudgmental way.

Seventy schools from across the country sent eighty-eight coaches for training during the summer of 1995. Each succeeding summer a comparable number of schools and coaches have joined the NSRF, which is now an independent organization housed at the Harmony Center in Bloomington, Indiana. The schools represent all regions of the country, all levels of students (K-12), all sizes of schools, and diversity in socioeconomic status and in racial and ethnic composition, and included urban, suburban, and rural schools.

A CFG meets at least once a month for at least two hours to work together on improving their teaching practice. For each meeting, the members select from a menu of NSRF-designed activities, such as analysis of student work, analysis of teacher work, discussions about an article or book they have read, or a debriefing of peer classroom observations.

Theory of Action. The NSRF developers' theory of action is as follows:

1. Teacher joins CFG.
2. Teacher engages in conversations about teaching and learning.
3. Teacher begins to think differently about his or her teaching.
4. Teacher decides to try a different way to teach.
5. Teacher tries a new way to teach.
6. Teacher invites CFG colleague to observe his or her new way of teaching.
7. Colleague offers candid but friendly feedback on what he or she observed.
8. Teacher realizes he or she was not doing what he or she thought he or she was.
9. Teacher tries again with colleague observing.
10. Colleague gives candid but friendly feedback on what he or she observed.
11. Numerous iterations of steps 2 through 10.
12. Teacher's pedagogy becomes more student centered.
13. Teacher's students begin achieving better.

This theory of action assumes that any of the CFG activities or types of conversations will lead the teachers to begin to think more deeply about their teaching, that is, to become more reflective.

During the first year of the project, the NSRF developers decided to fund a formal evaluation, retaining one of us (Bill Nave) to design and conduct the study. A randomized field trial was not an option for this evaluation for at least three reasons. First, the NSRF was not yet a mature program, because the developers continued to modify the criteria for selecting schools and the coaches' training as they learned from the first two groups of participants. Second, funding was insufficient to support a field trial. Third, the developers were not inclined to withhold the training from any school that met the criteria for acceptance into the program.

Therefore, Nave selected a theory-based evaluation design as the framework for the study. A theory-based evaluation carefully defines the theory of action of the program to be investigated and then systematically gathers data for each of the steps in the theory (Weiss, 1985, 1997a, 1997b, 1997c, 1998). Based on their first two years of experience with the program, the developers had clarified their expectations about the series of steps that would lead from the CFG discussions to improved teaching and learning.

The evaluation design covered two and a half school years and included the following strategies:

- Observations of CFG meetings to see what activities they used and what they discussed
- Classroom observations of CFG teachers to see how their teaching changed
- Interviews with CFG teachers to see how they think about their teaching and what activities they engage in between research visits
- Systematic collection of student work samples related to the CFG work
- Interviews with the CFG coaches and the schools' principals to understand the context of the work

Operation of a Typical CFG. We provide here a brief description of the CFG work at Beech Elementary School (a pseudonym) to demonstrate the program's function.[5] Beech's CFG teachers decided to focus on improving the writing skills of their third-, fourth-, and fifth-grade students. They used their CFG meetings to analyze samples of their students' writing, using the process that their state uses for scoring the annual writing exam for all fourth-, eighth-, and eleventh-grade students. After several meetings, one of the teachers commented that they were learning a lot about good student writing by using this state scoring process, and he suggested that their students would probably benefit from engaging in the same process. His colleagues agreed, and together they planned a set of lessons for their students to learn how to use the state's scoring process.

These CFG teachers taught their students how to apply the state scoring process using a set of student writing samples that their state department of education provided.[6] The teachers then gave their students a writing assignment and had them score their own papers. Next, the teachers had their students score the writing of other students in their class (anonymously, using photocopies with the students' names blacked out). After a few iterations of this process, the teachers began a series of exchanges, having students score papers from other classes. During this set of exchanges, the students provided written explanations for their scoring decisions as additional feedback to their peers in the other classes. After reading these explanations, several students requested that they be able to talk with the student who had scored their paper so they could have more detailed feedback in order to target their attempts better to improve their writing.

Responding to this request, the CFG teachers assigned another set of writing tasks, this time having students in two different classes score the same student's paper from a third class, then meet to discuss their scoring decisions before they both met with the paper's author. These face-to-face editing sessions among students continued through the balance of the school year, expanding to include cross-grade student editing sessions.

Results of the CFG Work. Ultimately it became time to evaluate the impact of this program on the CFG teachers.

Evaluation Evidence for Changes in Teachers. Analysis of the data from the twelve schools in the NSRF study support two assertions. First, in schools where the NSRF was faithfully implemented, the majority of CFG teachers changed the way they thought about their teaching. In general, they became more thoughtful about the connections among curriculum, instruction, and assessment. Second, in these same high-implementation schools, the majority of CFG teachers changed the way they taught, demonstrating more coherence among the components of their lessons and units (Nave, 1998, 2000a, 2000b).

Data from one of the twelve schools in the study provided an unexpected finding. All six teachers in the CFG changed their practice around the teaching of writing as they worked on this issue during their CFG meetings. Randomly selected student writing samples showed improvements in writing skills when analyzed according to the standards the teachers and students used as their guide to good writing. However, only three of the teachers seem to have become more reflective about their teaching practice. Interviews from the other three suggest that not only did they *not* change their thinking about their teaching, but they also asserted that their teaching practice with writing had not changed. These interview assertions directly contradict the classroom observations over two and a half years that record substantial changes in pedagogy in the writing curriculum for these teachers.

The value of supporting teachers to become more reflective about their teaching as a precursor to their decisions to make changes in their pedagogy seemed well supported in the research literature. However, evidence from the NSRF evaluation suggests that deeper teacher reflection may not be essential for improved practice. The three apparently nonreflective teachers at Beech Elementary changed their practice without first becoming more thoughtful. Perhaps for some teachers, the process of working with their colleagues around an issue of instruction is sufficient to change their practice.

This surprising finding was possible, in part at least, because of the design of a theory-based evaluation. Theory-based evaluations are designed to look for disconfirming evidence as well as confirmatory evidence about each of the steps in the theory of action of the program being studied.

Evaluation Evidence for Changes in Student Performance. The NSRF evaluation collected samples of student writing from six randomly selected students in each of the CFG teachers' classes at the beginning and the end of the second full year of the evaluation. Analysis of the samples with the state scoring process that the teachers and students were using as a guideline revealed substantial improvements in the students' writing skills. Writing samples of students in the CFG teachers' classes who had conducted more of the writing exchanges with other classes showed more improvement than the writing of students in classes participating in fewer of the exchanges.

Comparison of the Three Cases

The impact of evaluation findings depended on the management decisions in each of the school systems.

Leadership. In terms of the kind of leadership necessary to develop and sustain a district-wide faculty improvement program, the district leaders in Pittsburgh and New York City were there for over a decade, and their programs developed and matured over several years early in their tenure (Reports to the Ford Foundation I-VII, 1993–1989; Elmore and Burney, 1998). After Wallace retired, his systematic professional development initiatives in Pittsburgh ended. The Pittsburgh School Board changed the policy emphasis in the district to a focus on multiculturalism. On the other hand, the professional improvement programs in District Two continue even though Alvarado left at the end of school year 1997–1998 to become the chancellor of instruction for the San Diego Public Schools. The new superintendent of District Two—formerly Alvarado's deputy superintendent during his ten-year tenure—is experienced with the professional development programs and continues to support them.

In the NSRF program, the CFG teachers themselves were responsible for the continuous improvement of their instructional strategies. However, one school context factor in particular was strongly related to the success of the CFG work in changing teachers' thinking and practice. In schools where the CFG met during the school day, the principal was a member of the CFG, and participants used the CFG process to work on improving their practice, the CFG worked as designed, and the program consistently resulted in improvements in teachers' instructional practices. Conversely, in schools where the principal did not support the meetings during the school day and also was not a member of the group, the process was much more variable in its effect on teachers (Nave, 1998, 2000a, 2000b).

Evaluation Evidence for Changes in Teachers. Documentation about the Schenley High School Teacher Center reports only one study of changes in teachers' instructional behaviors. That study was small, involving only special education teachers who volunteered to participate (Zigmond, Kohnke, and Miller, 1986). We cannot generalize the results of the study to the rest of Pittsburgh's teachers. We have no other information about changes in teaching behaviors of any of the other approximately 910 teachers who spent their eight weeks at Schenley.

The material we have on District Two does not provide data about changes in teachers' instructional behaviors, so we cannot describe any changes in teachers' classroom skills there.

CFG teachers in the NSRF evaluation changed both the way they think about their teaching and their instructional practices. However, these changes depended on the degree of faithful implementation of the program model.

Evaluation Evidence for Changes in Students. The improvements in standardized test scores reported for Schenley and high schools across the district could have other explanations. For example, at Schenley itself, an entire new faculty selected from among the best teachers in the district taught the students beginning in September 1993. We would expect student test scores to reflect this change in staff. In addition, many new students enrolled at Schenley in response to the new magnet programs. These new students were likely to be better prepared than those already at Schenley, who had been scoring last among the district's high schools.

The other high schools in Pittsburgh also welcomed many new students returning from the city's Catholic parochial and other private schools. As at Schenley, these students were likely better prepared than the students who were already in the high schools. None of the documentation of the work of the teacher center provides data we could use to determine the differential effects on student test scores of a teacher's time at Schenley.

Such data require detailed record keeping, such as can be done with a digital management information system. During the late 1970s and early 1980s, researchers at the Learning Research and Development Center (LRDC) had been working with the Pittsburgh Public Schools to design and implement such a system. They had discovered that Pittsburgh's paper record-keeping system was so cumbersome and that some students moved so frequently that some schools in the district found it difficult to produce an accurate roster of their current students, much less a record of their students' achievement and test results over the years (Cooley and Bickel, 1986).

The first management information system in Pittsburgh proved so useful to the district central office staff that they used up much of the available computer memory and time on the system. The result was that principals in the schools had little access to the data in the system to inform their decisions in their schools. In response, LRDC began working on a second-generation system with separate computing capabilities at each school for principals, but that system was not in place at the time of the Schenley evaluation studies (Cooley and Bickel, 1986).

As was the case in Pittsburgh, possible alternative explanations exist for the improvement in student test scores in New York's District Two. Principals replaced half of District Two's teachers between 1987 and 1995. Alvarado's policy of accountability for both teachers and principals based on continuous improvement in teachers' instructional skills has likely motivated teachers to pay more attention to their instructional behaviors and to how well their students are learning. In addition, during Alvarado's tenure in District Two, middle-class students have been returning to the public schools from private schools (Elmore and Burney, 1998). As in Pittsburgh, these students are likely better prepared than other students and likely have had a positive impact on achievement test scores in District Two.

The NSRF study provides evidence of improved student learning in some skills in the classes of teachers in some of the CFGs. For example, the systematic collection of student work at Beech Elementary School revealed substantial improvements in the students' writing products (Nave, 2000b).

Conclusion

Precedent exists for launching ambitious, systematic, and large-scale professional development aimed at improving teachers' instructional skills and students' academic achievement. Those planning such programs need not begin from scratch; they can learn from evaluations of the impact of the work done in Pittsburgh, Community District Two, and the NCRF initiative.

Despite the ambitious scope of the Pittsburgh and New York City professional development programs, the evaluations tell us that their impact on teachers' skills or on student learning remains unclear. Both reported improvements in student test scores on standardized tests, but neither included a rigorous evaluation design from the outset that was tightly coupled with the two objectives of improving teacher skills and student achievement. The NSRF evaluation, on the other hand, was designed both to examine the impact of the program and provide data on the program's theory of action. Analysis of the data supports the assertions of changes in teachers as well as impact on student learning. These changes were related to the degree of faithful implementation of the NSRF theory. In schools where the CFGs met regularly and the teachers talked about ways to improve their instruction, more changes occurred in their practice (Nave, 2000b). The evaluation design also allowed a surprising finding to surface: that teachers can change their practice dramatically without first thinking more deeply about their teaching.

The inability to ascribe the improvements in student achievement to the two district programs underscores the importance of including careful evaluation planning at the beginning of a process of school improvement.

Notes

1. These case studies are based on several important sources. For the Schenley High School Teacher Center in Pittsburgh, we draw primarily from documents produced in the evaluation of the Schenley project, found in the archives of the Ford Foundation, which funded the Schenley evaluation study. We also found important data on the context of the Schenley work in Cooley and Bickel (1986) and in Wallace (1996). For the program in District Two we draw from work done by Elmore and Burney (1998, 1999), which included extensive fieldwork in District Two. For the NSRF program, we rely on Nave's evaluation (1998, 2000a, 2000b).

2. Data for the construction of this hypothetical visiting teacher experience come from several sources: (Davis, 1986; Reports to the Ford Foundation I–VI, 1983–1987).

3. Alvarado left District Two to become chancellor for instruction for the San Diego Public Schools during the summer of 1998.

4. Twenty-five percent of the national student normal population is in each quarter.

5. This description is based on the NSRF evaluation (Nave, 2000b).

6. This state's department of education provides photocopies of anonymous student writing samples from previous state exams to any teacher who requests them.

References

Cooley, W. W., and Bickel, W. E. *Decision Oriented Educational Research*. Boston: Kluwer-Nijhoff, 1986.

Davis, L. E. "A Recipe for the Development of an Effective Teaching Clinic." Paper presented at American Society for Child Development meeting, San Francisco, Mar. 1, 1986. (ED 275 028)

Elmore, R. F., and Burney, D. *Investing in Teacher Learning: Staff Development and Instructional Improvement: Community District #2, New York City*. Washington, D.C.: National Commission on Teaching and America's Future, Consortium for Policy Research in Education, 1998. (ED 416 203)

Elmore, R. F., and Burney, D. *School Variation and Systemic Instructional Improvement in Community School District #2, New York City*. Cambridge, Mass.: High Performance Learning Communities Project, 1999. (ED 429 264)

Hunter, M. *Mastery Teaching*. El Segundo, Calif.: TIP Publications, 1982.

McLaughlin, M. M., and Talbert, J. E. "The Contexts in Question: The Secondary School Workplace." In M. W. McLaughlin, J. E. Talbert, and N. Bascia (eds.), *The Contexts of Teaching in Secondary Schools: Teachers' Realities*. New York: Teachers College Press, 1990.

McLaughlin, M. M., and Talbert, J. E. *Contexts That Matter for Teaching and Learning*. Stanford, Calif.: Center for Research on the Context of Secondary School Teaching, Stanford University, 1993.

Memorandum of Understanding Between Pittsburgh Board and Pittsburgh Federation of Teachers Concerning Teacher Center. 1982. Ford Foundation Archives. New York. (Grant PA 08201071)

Moore-Johnson, S. *Teachers at Work: Achieving Success in Our Schools*. New York: Basic Books, 1990.

Nave, B. *National School Reform Faculty Program Evaluation: First Year Report to Schools*. Providence, R.I.: Brown University, 1998.

Nave, B. *Critical Friends Groups: Their Impact on Students, Teachers, and Schools: Results of a Two Year Qualitative Study of the National School Reform Faculty Program*. Annenberg Institute for School Reform. Providence, R.I.: Brown University, 2001.

Nave, B. "Among Critical Friends: A Study of Critical Friends Groups in Three Maine Schools." Unpublished doctoral dissertation, Harvard University, 2000b.

Report to the Ford Foundation I. Schenley High School Teacher Center. 1983. Ford Foundation Archives. New York. (Grant PA 08201071)

Report to the Ford Foundation II. Schenley High School Teacher Center. 1984. Ford Foundation Archives, New York. (Grant PA 08201071)

Report to the Ford Foundation III. Schenley High School Teacher Center. 1984. Ford Foundation Archives, New York. (Grant PA 08201071)

Report to the Ford Foundation IV. Schenley High School Teacher Center. 1985. Ford Foundation Archives, New York. (Grant PA 08201071)

Report to the Ford Foundation V. Schenley High School Teacher Center. 1986. Ford Foundation Archives, New York. (Grant PA 08201071)

Report to the Ford Foundation VI. Schenley High School Teacher Center. 1987. Ford Foundation Archives, New York. (Grant PA 08201071)

Report to the Ford Foundation VII. Schenley High School Teacher Center. 1989. Ford Foundation Archives, New York. (Grant PA 08201071)

Teacher Center Proposal to Ford Foundation for November 1983 to October 1988. 1982. Ford Foundation Archives, New York. (Grant PA 08201071)

Wallace, R. C. 1996. *From Vision to Practice: The Art of Educational Leadership*. Thousand Oaks, Calif.: Corwin Press, 1996.

Wallace, R., and others. "Secondary Education Renewal in Pittsburgh." *Educational Leadership*, 1984, *41*(6), 73–77.

Weiss, C. "Nothing as Practical as Good Theory: Exploring Theory-Based Evaluation for Comprehensive Community Initiatives for Children and Families." In J. P. Connell, A. C. Kubisch, L. B. Schorr, and C. H. Weiss (eds.), *New Approaches to Evaluating Community Initiatives. Concepts, Methods, and Contexts*. Washington, D.C.: Aspen Institute. 1985.

Weiss, C. "Bringing Theory-Based Evaluation Within Our Means." Working paper, Harvard Project on Schooling and Children, 1997a.

Weiss, C. "How Can Theory-Based Evaluation Make Greater Headway?" *Evaluation Review*, 1997b, *21*(4), 501–524.

Weiss, C. (ed.). *Theory-Based Evaluation: Past, Present, and Future*. New Directions for Evaluation, no. 76. San Francisco: Jossey-Bass, 1997c.

Weiss, C. *Evaluation: Methods for Studying Programs and Policies*. Englewood Cliffs, N.J.: Prentice Hall, 1998.

Zigmond, N., Kohnke, R., and Miller, S. "Assessing the Impact of Teacher Inservice on Secondary Special Education Classrooms." Paper presented at the American Educational Research Association meeting, San Francisco, Apr. 1986.

EDWARD MIECH is an associate of the Center for Evaluation, the Children's Initiative, American Academy of Arts and Sciences.

BILL NAVE is an associate of the Center for Evaluation, the Children's Initiative, American Academy of Arts and Sciences.

FREDERICK MOSTELLER is professor emeritus of statistics and health policy and management at Harvard University and director of the Center for Evaluation of the Children's Initiative at the American Academy of Arts and Sciences.

Name Index

Abrahamse, A., 18
Adorno, T., 28
Almario, D. A., 41
Altenbaugh, R. J., 71, 76, 78
Alton-Lee, A., 72, 73
Alvarado, A., 88, 89, 90, 95, 96
Annan, S., 12, 16
Astin, A. W., 71

Barbacci, M., 49
Barnett, W. S., 66
Bartels, L., 31
Battaglia, F., 41
Bell, W. C., 45
Beriama, 21
Berk, R. A., 10, 11, 13, 14, 15, 17, 18, 19, 62
Bickel, W. E., 96
Bijker, W., 28
Birkhead, G. S., 47
Black, H., 11, 17
Blackstone, E., 31
Blakely, E., 26
Blumstein, A., 12, 15, 18
Bobadilla, J. L., 56
Boffey, P., 11
Boruch, 21
Boughton, P., 32
Bourke-White, M., 79
Brookmeyer, R., 41
Bruner, J. S., 79
Burney, D., 84, 89, 90, 91, 95, 96

Cain, G., 66
Campbell, A., 17, 18, 19
Carlson, K., 18
Carson, B. H., 71
Chaisson, R. E., 49
Chalk, R., 1, 4, 9, 12, 13, 17, 19
Ching, S., 45
Clune, W., 60
Cohen, J., 12, 15, 18
Cohen, M. A., 9
Cohn, E., 10, 11
Coleman, J. S., 58
Coleman, S., 70
Conway, M. A., 73
Cooley, W. W., 96

Cordray, D., 19
Cotrell, H. W., 74
Cotton, D., 41
Csikszentmihalyi, M., 71, 77
Cunningham, W., 25, 26, 27, 31, 32
Curtin, S. C., 43
Cu-Uvin, S., 41

Daughtry, S., 31
Davidson, E. C., 41
Davis, L. E., 86
Davis, M., 26, 27
Davis, S. F., 42, 47
de Tocqueville, A., 28, 30
Dean, C. W., 15
Divack, A., 83
Douglas, S., 28
Drew, C. R., 41
Driver, C., 61
Drummond, M. F., 56, 60
Dunford, F. W., 12, 14, 15

Eddy, D. M., 56
Ellin, N., 26
Elliott, D. S., 12, 14, 15
Elmore, R. F., 84, 89, 90, 91, 95, 96
Emerson, J., 83
Erhlich, I., 18
Evans, P., 18

Fantuzzo, J. W., 21
Farrington, D., 10
Fink, A., 62
Fischer, C., 28, 29
Flanagan, J., 18
Fleming, P. L., 42
Flusty, S., 26
Forrester, J., 29
Freeman, H. E., 62

Garner, J., 1, 4, 10, 12, 13, 15, 16, 17, 19
Gartin, P. R., 14
George, D. A., 31
Glass, G. V., 61, 64, 65
Glendon, M. A., 39
Gold, M. R., 56, 60
Goldman, K., 45

SUBJECT INDEX

Arrest for domestic violence, evaluating: challenges of, 19–20; Charlotte experiment, 15; Colorado Springs experiment, 16–17; conflicting findings in, 4, 12; Dade County experiment, 16; history of, 10–11; Milwaukee experiment, 15–16; Minneapolis study, 4, 10–11, 13–14, 20; Omaha study, 14–15; qualitative and quantitative approaches in, 17–19; replication research, 11–12; and study design, 12–17; value of, 20–21

Autobiographical memory research: college memories, 74–75; conclusions on, 80–81; for improving educational evaluations, 69, 73–74; for improving pedagogy, 76–78; as qualitative data for educators, 6–7, 70–71; and student success, 78–80, 81; test performance and memory, 71–73

Common wisdoms, challenging, 1–8
Conflicting findings, interpreting, 4
Contamination stories, 80
Cost-effectiveness analyses: defined, 57–58; in education, 6, 55–66; in HIV prevention, 5–6, 46–48

Domestic violence, prevalence of, 9
Domestic violence studies: challenges in, 19–20; Charlotte experiment, 15; Colorado Springs experiment, 16–17; conflicting findings in, 4, 12; Dade County experiment, 16; design of, 12–17; history of police arrest studies, 10–11; Milwaukee experiment, 15–16; Minneapolis study, 4, 10–11, 13–14, 20; Omaha study, 14–15; qualitative and quantitative approaches in, 17–19; replication research, 11–12; value of, 20–21

Education, cost-effectiveness analyses in: conclusions on, 64–66; dearth of, 57, 58–61; defined, 57–58; importance of,

55–56; lack of demand for, 63–64; training for, 61–62

Educational evaluations, memory research data in: college memories, 74–75; conclusions on, 80–81; for pedagogical improvement, 76–78; questions addressed by, 69; and student success, 78–80, 81; and test performance, 71–73; test scores versus, 70–71

Educational evaluations of teachers: comparison of 3 cases, 95–97; conclusions on, 97; in New York City, 84, 88–91; in NRSF* program, 84–85, 91–94; overview of, 83–84; in Pittsburgh, 84, 85–88

HIV prevention, perinatal: cost-effective analyses of, 5–6, 46–48; evaluation of efforts in, 44–48; recommendations for, 49–50; targeted approach to, 41–43; value of IOM report on, 50–51

Home security, privatization of: common wisdom on, 5, 25, 26–27; conclusions about, 36–37; questions for evaluating, 27–30; surprising findings on, 30–35

Intimate partner violence studies: challenges in, 19–20; Charlotte experiment, 15; Colorado Springs experiment, 16–17; conflicting findings in, 4, 12; Dade County experiment, 16; history of arrest studies, 10–11; Milwaukee experiment, 15–16; Minneapolis study, 4, 10–11, 13–14, 20; Omaha study, 14–15; qualitative and quantitative approaches in, 17–19; replication research, 11–12; and study design, 12–17; value of, 20–21

Memory research, autobiographical: college memories, 74–75; conclusions on, 80–81; for educational evaluation improvement, 69, 73–74; for pedagogical improvement, 76–78; as qualitative data for educators, 6–7, 70–71;

*National School Reform Faculty program

105

*National School Reform Faculty program

Back Issue/Subscription Order Form

Copy or detach and send to:

Jossey-Bass Inc., Publishers, 350 Sansome Street, San Francisco CA 94104-1342

Call or fax toll free!

Phone 888-378-2537 6AM-5PM PST; Fax 800-605-2665

Back issues: Please send me the following issues at $27 each.

(Important: please include series initials and issue number, such as EV77.)

1. EV _____

_____

_____

$ _____ Total for single issues

$ _____ Shipping charges (for single issues *only;* subscriptions are exempt from shipping charges): Up to $30, add $5^{50} • $30^{01}–$50, add $6^{50} $50^{01}–$75, add $7^{50} • $75^{01}–$100, add $9 • $100^{01}–$150, add $10 Over $150, call for shipping charge.

Subscriptions Please ❑ start ❑ renew my subscription to *New Directions for Evaluation* for the year ___ at the following rate:

❑ Individual: $66 U.S./Canada/Mexico; $90 International

❑ Institutional: $130 U.S.; $170 Canada; $204 International

NOTE: Subscriptions are quarterly, and are for the calendar year only. Subscriptions begin with the spring issue of the year indicated above. For shipping outside the U.S., please add $25. Prices are subject to change.

$ _____ Total single issues and subscriptions (CA, IN, NJ, NY and DC residents, add sales tax for single issues. NY and DC residents must include shipping charges when calculating sales tax. NY and Canadian residents only, add sales tax for subscriptions.)

❑ Payment enclosed (U.S. check or money order only.)

❑ VISA, MC, AmEx, Discover Card #_____ Exp. date_____

Signature _____ Day phone _____

❑ Bill me (U.S. institutional orders only. Purchase order required.)

Purchase order #_____

Name _____

Address _____

_____

Phone_____ E-mail _____

For more information about Jossey-Bass Publishers, visit our Web site at:

www.josseybass.com **PRIORITY CODE = ND1**

Evaluation Findings That Surprise
Richard J. Light (ed.)
New Directions for Evaluation, no. 90
Jennifer C. Greene, Gary T. Henry, Coeditors-in-Chief
Copyright ©2000 Jossey-Bass, A Publishing Unit of John Wiley & Sons, Inc.

Microfilm copies of issues and articles are available in 16mm and 35mm, as well as microfiche in 105mm, through University Microfilms Inc., 300 North Zeeb Road, Ann Arbor, Michigan 48106-1346.

New Directions for Evaluation is indexed in Contents Pages in Education, Higher Education Abstracts, and Sociological Abstracts.

ISSN 1097-6736   ISBN 0-7879-5792-5

NEW DIRECTIONS FOR EVALUATION is part of The Jossey-Bass Education Series and is published quarterly by Jossey-Bass, 350 Sansome Street, San Francisco, California 94104-1342.

SUBSCRIPTIONS cost $66.00 for U.S./Canada/Mexico; $90 international. For institutions, agencies, and libraries, $130 U.S.; $170 Canada; $204 international. Prices subject to change.

EDITORIAL CORRESPONDENCE should be addressed to the Editors-in-Chief, Jennifer C. Greene, Department of Educational Psychology, University of Illinois, 260E Education Building, 1310 South Sixth Street, Champaign, IL 61820, or Gary T. Henry, School of Policy Studies, Georgia State University, P.O. Box 4039, Atlanta, GA 30302-4039.

www.josseybass.com

2002

NEW DIRECTIONS FOR EVALUATION
A PUBLICATION OF THE AMERICAN EVALUATION ASSOCIATION

Gary T. Henry, *Georgia State University*
COEDITOR-IN-CHIEF

Jennifer C. Greene, *University of Illinois*
COEDITOR-IN-CHIEF

Evaluation Findings That Surprise

Richard J. Light
Harvard University

EDITOR

Number 90, Summer 2001

JOSSEY-BASS
San Francisco